Rip's depot. The narrow gauge penetrated deep into Washington Irving country. The background mountains were the legendary home of Rip's little men. *(Adrienne White Lightbourne Collection, courtesy of Mabel Parker Smith)*

RIP VAN WINKLE RAILROADS

RIP VAN WINKLE RAILROADS

By William F. Helmer

CANAJOHARIE & CATSKILL R.R.
CATSKILL MOUNTAIN RY.
OTIS ELEVATING RY.
CATSKILL & TANNERSVILLE RY.

BERKELEY Howell -North Books CALIFORNIA

RIP VAN WINKLE RAILWAYS

Printed and bound in the United States of America

Library of Congress Catalog Card No. 77-116732

ISBN 0-8310-7079-X

Published by Howell-North Books
1050 Parker Street, Berkeley, California 94710

For My Parents

Acknowledgments

The following persons have generously made available to me the resources of their respective institutions: Donald Sinclair, the Library of Rutgers, the State University; Charles E. Dornbusch and Raymond Beecher, the Vedder Memorial Library; Bruce R. Brown, Colgate University Library; the late Eugene J. Magner and Michael Gieryic, SUNY College at Morrisville Library; John White, Jr., United States National Museum; Vernon Haskins, Durham Center Museum; Harry Eddy, Bureau of Railway Economics Library; James Heslin, New-York Historical Society; Robert T. Treese, University of Michigan Library; Mary Roy, Northwestern University Library; Dorothy Augustine, Catskill Public Library; Juliet Wolohan, New York State Library; Kathleen Dowling, Jervis Library Association; Clifford K. Shipton and Marcus A. McCorison, the American Antiquarian Society and Leon deValinger, Delaware State Archives.

These individuals have contributed to this work their knowledge of these railroads or pertinent material from their collections: Mabel Parker Smith (Greene County Historian), Barbara Rivette, Karl Korbel, George Holdridge, Howard Muller, George Phelps, Harold K. Vollrath, T. J. Sheehey, Winfield W. Robinson, Iva E. Cammer, Charles Cammer, Walter Bliss, Richard Palmer, Edward Baumgardner, Edward Bond, Alan Ruf, Emily Carl, J. Burgett Wolcott, Alexander Phillips, Harry E. Jones, William P. Coffin, Elmer Mower, Carol Memmen, Milton Wagenfohr, Mary Rising, Robert Dineen, Robert F. Harding, Beatrice Adams, Eleanor J. Beach, Jean Sidar, Gerald M. Best, Edward Vogel, Dale Stein, the late A. Fred Saunders and the late Arthur C. Mack.

While it would be foolhardy to attempt to thank all of these men and women for their substantial individual contributions, at least five deserve special recognition: Edward P. Baumgardner has been a constant source of inspiration and information, Mabel Parker Smith has provided quantities of factual material, Vernon Haskins has lent his special regional expertise to my quest, Raymond Beecher has provided access to the Vedder Memorial Library at my convenience (not always at his) and Harry E. Jones has supplied much first-hand knowledge of the later railroads.

For their assistance, I am truly grateful. And if, in the four years of amassing Catskilliana or during the final days of manuscript preparation, I have overlooked names which should be included in this place, I apologize to those persons. Certainly no omission was intended.

I have been fortunate in obtaining the services of a fine artist, Manville B. Wakefield, whose map work and painting for this volume can only add to his reputation for excellence. And Mr. and Mrs. Morgan North deserve my gratitude for their patience, guidance and good-natured prodding. Mrs. Sharon Ogrydziak deserves more credit than is usual for typists; only one who has seen the original handwriting could appreciate her achievement.

Work on this book has been facilitated by the aid furnished by the Research Foundation of State University of New York. The Foundation's continuing support of my study of the state's abandoned railroads has been most gratifying. Completion of the manuscript was made possible by a sabbatical leave graciously granted by President Whipple of the College and Chancellor Gould of the State University of New York.

Last of all, I want to express my appreciation to Billy, Steve, Mary Claire and Mike for heeding their mother's instruction: "Quiet, please! Daddy is working!" Their occasional observance of the warning has been sufficient to get this book finished.

WILLIAM F. HELMER

State University Agricultural & Technical College
Morrisville, New York 13408

Contents

The Canajoharie and Catskill Rail Road Company.

No.

New=York, 183

Be it known, *That* is

entitled to SHARES *in the Capital*

Stock of the **Canajoharie and Catskill Rail Road Company,** *upon*

which there has been paid *Dollars*

on each Share of Fifty Dollars.

This Certificate is transferable on the Books of the Company only,
and on its delivery by the said
or *Attorney.*

President.

Secretary.

TIME TABLE IN EFFECT JUNE 27, 1905

Direct and Favorite
Route to the
Catskill Mountains

=Catskill Mountain,=
=Otis and=
Catskill & Tannersville
=Railways=

C. A. BEACH, Gen'l Supt. C. M. Ry.
J. L. DRISCOLL, Supt. O. and C. & T. Rys.
T. E. JONES, Gen'l Passenger Agent C. M. Ry.
CATSKILL, N. Y.

Preface

In the history of American railroading, forty years of operation seems a brief span indeed. The student of transportation can rapidly calculate that just so many years separate the introduction of steam railroading into the United States from the completion of the first transcontinental line. This period, from the STOURBRIDGE LION's cautious journey over the Delaware & Hudson Canal Company's light trackage to the rowdy celebration around the head-to-head locomotives at Promontory Point, is but the opening act in the drama of American railroading. The account which follows covers an identical number of years, but chronicles no such momentous events. It does not even contain the memoirs of a single corporation; the railroad projects are separated in time by almost half a century. Yet all this activity galvanized an entire New York State county, exploited the picturesque Catskill mountain range and terminated at a single Hudson River port, Catskill.

These forty years offer a fine insight into two exciting eras in American transportation history — the feverish pioneer railroad epoch and the golden age of narrow gauge. The Canajoharie & Catskill underwent all the tribulations of the earliest trial-and-error, hit-or-miss kind of operation characteristic of the new mode of communication and succumbed; the Catskill narrow gauge lines experimented with the light railway and failed. The C. & C. lived out its brief life as a freight carrier; the later lines courted passengers almost exclusively. Both served their time and then vanished. Nevertheless, in their struggle for survival, they serve as models for what was best — and what was worst — in American railroading.

Although the stories presented here are as complete and as accurate as I can make them, there are tantalizing questions remaining. The surviving records of the Canajoharie & Catskill are scarce and scattered, arousing curiosity not only as to the everyday operating problems of the railroad, but about the critical deliberations of its beleaguered officials. Apparently all of the company's books and papers have been lost or destroyed. Fortunately, the more recent carriers are represented by some company documents resurrected from a Catskill garage. Yet even these are fragmentary.

The person interested in America's past must deplore the too-casual discarding of old pictures, minute books, maps, diaries, letters, timetables and other railroad memorabilia. Much of value has been lost, but some undoubtedly remains, hidden or forgotten in the nooks and crannies of our domestic and business structures.

Therefore, the conscientious attic cleaner will want to consult his nearest historical library or museum before such materials are dumped or burned. And I will be glad to hear of any discoveries related to my work on the railroads of New York State.

ch'd by J. Glennie Esq.   *Hewi*

Catskill Mountains and the Steam Boat — on the Hudson River.

Catskill Mountains and the Steam Boat. This somewhat romantic engraving by Hewitt from a J. Glennie sketch appeared in *The Portfolio* for November, 1813. The sharply-pointed peaks represent pure artistic license, but the view is not too dissimilar to that seen by Washington Irving and other river travelers. *(Library of Congress Collection)*

CHAPTER ONE

Rip's Realm

NOTHING could seem more out of time and place than a railway train clanking through the placid Dutch New York village that Washington Irving chose as the home of Rip Van Winkle. Yet not long after the celebrated tale appeared in print, in many little hamlets under the brow of the Catskill Mountains, the Canajoharie & Catskill Rail Road laid its strap-iron rails. And while Irving's creation was still fresh in the American public imagination, a whole system of narrow gauge railroads entered into the very heart of Rip Van Winkle's territory. Palenville, the most likely candidate for the honor of harboring the Van Winkle clan, became a terminal for the Catskill Mountain Railway in 1882.

Before this rude invasion, the purple-shrouded Catskill peaks were mysterious and romantic precincts to be gazed at from the decks of sloops and steamers plying the Hudson River between New York and Albany. At the time he wrote the story, Irving himself had not stood closer to his imagined scenes than this. The inner regions of the Catskill Mountains remained a kind of *terra incognita* on the North American continent. Travelers by land took the easier level roads to the West; settlers in the Hudson Valley formed a semi-circle of homesteads around the eastern base of the precipice. At the steep face of the mountains, the solid barrier that the Indians called the "Wall of Manitou," the domesticated land stopped. Only hunters, trappers, a few independent farmers and other hardy types ventured into the wooded heights west of the Hudson.

Then, in 1823, a group of businessmen from the village of Catskill opened a door to the mountains. The Catskill Mountain Association started the movement that would make the Catskills into a favored resort for vacationers from the crowded cities, and, especially, from the City of New York. Purchasing some of the wild property known as Pine Orchard, a vantage point located between North and South Mountains, the Association erected a modest guest house exploiting a panoramic view of the Hudson Valley. From this outlook James Fenimore Cooper's Leatherstocking is believed to have seen "all creation," and it was not far from the site of Henry David Thoreau's visit, before he took up his residence at Walden Pond. Thoreau described his visit briefly but well:

> I lodged at the house of a saw-miller last summer, on the Catskill Mountains, high up as Pine Orchard, in the blueberry and raspberry region, where the quiet and cleanliness and coolness seemed to be all one,—which had their ambrosial character. . . . The house seemed high-placed, airy, and perfumed, fit to entertain a travelling god. It was so high, indeed, that all the music, the broken strains, the waifs and accompaniments of tunes, that swept over the ridge of the Catskills, passed through its aisles. Could not man be man in such an abode?[1]

When the Catskill Mountain House grew from the Association's first structure, the locale became famous throughout the East.[2]

By 1836, the ledge on which it stood was receiving regular and enthusiastic notice in descriptive works:

> The prospect from this rock is more expansive and diversified than, perhaps, from any other point in the United States. Petty inequalities disappear, and the whole surrounding country is spread out as a plain. The eye roves in endless gratification, over farms, villages, towns, and cities, stretching between the Green Mountains of Vermont on the N. and the Highlands.[3]

The endless gratification extended also to the promoters of such a bountiful natural resource, which drew larger numbers of summer visitors in each succeeding year. Employment was found for many local residents, not only at the hotel itself, but on the wagons and coaches which loaded foodstuffs and sundries, passengers and baggage from the docks at Catskill village for delivery at the top of the mountains.

Some of the earliest visitors to the rock outcropping upon which the Catskill Mountain House arose were determined to put this magnificent scenery onto canvas. Striding on foot along rock-strewn paths or jouncing in buggies up primitive roads came the first members of the Hudson River School of American painting. The same romantic impulse that had given life to "Rip Van Winkle" also inspired magnificent landscapes from the brushes of Thomas Cole, Thomas Doughty, Asher B. Durand, J. F. Kensett and other talented limners. The Catskill peaks furnished these painters with both the subjects and the vantage points for their artistic endeavors. For a time it appeared that these mountains and these mountains alone might become the focal point for the budding artistic and literary enterprises in the new nation.

And another, less sophisticated, commodity was becoming important in the Catskill forests. Taking advantage of the vast stands of hemlock, the bark of which yielded the essential tannin for converting raw hides into leather, the tanners moved in. In 1818 the New York Tannery was shipping its first sides of sole leather from the village of Hunter. At first operated by William Edwards and his son, the business soon enlisted the talents of Jacob Lorillard and became one of the largest operations in the state. But soon the production of the Mammoth Tannery in nearby Prattsville was meeting and beating the competition. Here Zadock Pratt's three hundred vats are reported to have turned out one million sides of sole leather over a twenty-year period. In the process, 150,000 cords of hemlock bark were consumed.[4] Woodcutters and barkpeelers felled and stripped so many hemlocks in such thorough fashion that today the *Tsuga canadensis* is a scarce item in the Catskill forest. But the hundreds of tanneries which sprung up among the evergreen boughs demanded this tribute.

The abundant waterpower available along the Catskill Creek also attracted early industry. In 1836, along its banks or on its tributaries, in a distance of about 27 miles, there were 16 grist mills, 26 sawmills, 8 fulling mills, 7 carding machines, 1 woolen factory, 2 iron works, 1 trip hammer, 10 tanneries, 2 paper mills and 1 brewery. In that same year the port of Catskill shipped a quarter million sides of sole leather, three million feet of lumber and substantial quantities of butter, shingles, wool, tallow, hay and potash.[5] But Catskill and Greene County hankered for more.

Ever since the completion of the Erie Canal, in 1825, the uneasy residents had seen more and more water traffic moving north past their docks. The new inland waterway provided the state with a single thoroughfare from the port of New York to the West, making Buffalo and Cleveland heads of water navigation; no longer were the established turnpikes from Newburgh, Kingston and Catskill so attractive to travelers and shippers. The old river port of Catskill soon felt the impact. Although local trade remained stable, the turnpike did not prosper. Looking at the phenomenal growth in size and prosperity of Cleveland and Buffalo, or even at the steadily-increasing coal traffic over the Delaware & Hudson Canal at neighboring Kingston, the Catskill business community considered itself challenged and threatened. One of the first distinctions Catskill claimed was its strategic position on the Susquehanna Turnpike, a main route from New England to western New York and the frontier. When this communications artery suffered a diminished flow of goods and people, local pride and local pocketbooks felt the pain.

In order to counteract this morbid condition, citizens of Catskill banded together to protect their vital interests. The Catskill Mountain Association was already exploiting the tourist trade and doing it handily. To this effort was added a startling, almost revolutionary, plan to build a railroad paralleling the Susquehanna Turnpike.

One of the earliest railroad charters granted by the State of New York was the April 21, 1828 document creating the Catskill and Ithaca Rail Road.

The incorporators were Thomas B. Cooke, Orrin Day and Jacob Haight of Catskill, the easterly termination, and Francis Bloodgood, Jeremiah Beebe and Ebenezer Mack of Ithaca, its westernmost point. At Ithaca, publisher Mack was agitating for a connecting waterway through Cayuga Lake to Erie water and, ultimately, to Lake Ontario at Sodus Point.[6] From Ithaca south, local promoters projected the Ithaca and Owego, form-

The Catskills: Sunrise from South Mountain. William Cullen Bryant's *American Scenery* included this Harry Fenn illustration which emphasizes the panoramic view from the Catskill Mountain escarpment. *(Collection of the author)*

An early map of the Canajoharie & Catskill Rail Road. Representative of the inaccurate contemporary maps of the railroad is this projected line contained in T. G. Bradford's 1838 atlas. Because the company records have been lost, no reliable route map can now be found. *(New York State Library)*

ing a connection with the navigable Susquehanna River. The scope of the Catskill to Ithaca venture alone was enormous; not until 1853 did a single railroad line span the distance between the Hudson River and Cayuga Lake. And this mileage was formed from several independent companies which consolidated as the New York Central.

Nevertheless, Cooke, Mack and associates applied for federal assistance under the Survey Act of 1824 (which authorized the assignment of Army Engineer officers to investigate routes for canals, roads and railroads) and Lieutenant William Henry Swift began his topographical surveys from Ithaca to Catskill and from Ithaca to Owego. On the two projects he expended $2,538.61 and issued an Owego report late in 1828. The Catskill investigation took much longer, so much longer that the commissioners of the Catskill & Ithaca petitioned for an extension of time to complete the work and take subscriptions to the stock.[7] There were indications that formidable natural obstacles had been discovered between the two points.

The charter itself reflected turnpike practice, as did most pioneer railroad charters: it stipulated that "tolls" could be collected from travelers "with suitable and proper carriages." This kind of operation was impractical, of course, and all later charters eliminated the potentially troublesome reference. What was more revealing of an actual fact-of-life was the wording of a report which accompanied the enabling bill's introduction on March 27th:

> The route of the contemplated improvement lies through the southern tier of counties, a section of the state which has not yet participated in the benefits conferred by our grand system of internal improvement. While in other more favored districts, the public treasure has been expended with a liberal hand, this section has enjoyed no advantages, except such as nature afforded, or the industry and exertions of its inhabitants have supplied.[8]

Similarly, inhabitants of Hudson village, across the river from Catskill, yearned for the increase in business a railroad might supply.

While the Hudson & Berkshire company had no apparent contractual connection with the Catskill & Ithaca, an informal understanding must have been reached. For the Hudson project, surveyed from the riverport to the Massachusetts state line would there link up with the Western Railroad of Massachusetts and thus run to the seaport of Boston. A short trip by water from Hudson to Catskill would link the Atlantic Ocean with Western New York and the frontier. The Erie Canal would be circumvented and the Susquehanna Turnpike would be supplanted.

Substantial support was enlisted in the projects, but one prominent figure appeared in the Catskill venture — Thomas Burrage Cooke, sometime produce merchant, hardware dealer, justice of the peace, water freighter, bank president, Bible Society founder, and member of both the New York State Assembly and the United States House of Representatives.[9] His name became almost synonymous with the railroad in Greene County. Even though the rail-line to Ithaca was never built, an alternate route to Canajoharie was selected and Cooke became its tireless promoter.

Thus, less than twenty years after the creation of the Rip Van Winkle legend, Thomas B. Cooke and his associates began the massive invasion of the Catskill Mountains. The acrid fumes from the tanners' vats were already rising through the treetops. The proprietors of the Catskill Mountain House were carting junketeers and sightseers high onto the mountain, foreshadowing the annual migration that persists to this day. But symbolic of the great civilizing change was the appearance of the first railroad locomotive in this still romantic setting. Indeed, it even intruded into the consciousness of a great landscape artist.

The leader of the Hudson River School, Thomas Cole, concentrated his artistic talent upon the untamed natural scenery of the Catskills; the sharp rock outcroppings, the unkempt pine and hemlock forests, the plunging mountain streams, the ragged cloves and, of course, the shadowy summits themselves. The wonder is, then, that one of his later canvases recognized and illustrated the intrusion of the railway into the back country, infringing on Rip Van Winkle's territory, crowding close to the steep Catskill mountainsides. His fine painting, *River in the Catskills*, acknowledges the smoky presence of the Canajoharie & Catskill Rail Road; the slim embankment brings an unfamiliar precision to the untended land.

The machine had come to the wilderness.

Detail from Thomas Cole's *River in the Catskills*, c. 1841. The founder of the Hudson River School of painting depicted the passage of a Canajoharie & Catskill train over Jefferson Flat. There is no other known portrait of this equipment and, unfortunately, the locomotive and several cars are hidden from our sight. *(Courtesy M. and M. Karolik Collection, Museum of Fine Arts, Boston)*

17

CHAPTER TWO

Tom Cooke & Co., Railroad Builders

ECAUSE the Catskill & Ithaca plan was too far ahead of its time, it lost momentum after a fitful two years. A more modest project succeeded it. Thus, the Canajoharie & Catskill Rail Road began its corporate existence on April 19, 1830. Numbered among the promoters were Thomas B. Cooke and Jacob Haight, as well as two substantial citizens of Canajoharie, Henry Lieber and George Spraker. The line chosen for this new railroad was the shorter of two turnpikes to the West, calculated to achieve the same end as the earlier projection of a line of rails to Ithaca. The end, of course, was to capture some of the through freight and passenger traffic on the Hudson that was now by-passing the port of Catskill. Not only would it be a shortcut to the frontier, but it would be a channel of trade for the "interior" towns inconveniently distant from both the Hudson and the Erie.

On May 14th, orders were issued to Lieutenant John Pickell of the Army's 4th Artillery Regiment to go on topographical duty. All during the summer and early fall, the lieutenant and his men ranged the territory between the two points. By November 3rd he had completed his report on the Canajoharie to Catskill survey, in which he enthusiastically endorsed the venture. Such a railway, he said, would save travel time, it would avoid the ice which remained in the shadow of the Canal's "nose" east of Canajoharie and it would take advantage of the open water at Catskill when Albany was iced in three weeks earlier in the fall and three weeks later in the spring.[1]

One natural barrier, the heights south of Canajoharie, required Pickell to run three separate surveys, but in each case, he believed that an inclined plane would be necessary. In four other locations — at Flat Creek, north of Sloansville, over Stony Creek and at the village of Madison (now Leeds) —

the same kind of construction seemed to be called for. These sections would probably be powered by stationary steam engines which would draw the railway cars up the slope (although Pickell did not rule out possible use of horse power nor the use of water power in the one location where the fall of water was of sufficient volume and force — at Madison). During a part of his trek, Pickell noted the close company of Judge Thomas B. Cooke. The cost of construction for a single track line he estimated to be about $700,000.[2]

In order to have another expert opinion, President Cooke and his directors charged a noted civil engineer, William Gibbs McNeill, with the task of resurveying the entire route. While McNeill found little fault with the previous report, he was able to eliminate one inclined plane at Madison. He also added two miles to the road's length in order to modify the grades. His calculation of the cost was approximately $670,000.[3]

Assigned to assist McNeill were several engineers: Messrs. Root, Fessenden, Johnson, White, Schenck and Beach. Strengthening McNeill's final report was a supporting statement by Benjamin Wright, chief engineer of the Erie and Delaware & Hudson canals. Added to this solid backing was an optimistic letter signed by Ephraim William Beach, Engineer, in which he envisioned branch railroads along the various intersected valleys — all sending their manufactures and agricultural products to the Hudson River port of Catskill.[4] Expanding upon this proposal, apparently with the encouragement of Cooke, Beach then published a pamphlet calculated to inspire confidence in the C. & C. project. The title itself was a skillful bit of persuasion: *Remarks, Accompanied with a Letter of Report of Capt. E. Beach, Engineer, on the Feasibility of a Railroad Intersecting the Canajoharie and Catskill Railroad, and Extending Along the Valley of the Susquehannah, and from Thence to Lake Erie: With the Opinion of Benjamin Wright, Esq., Civil Engineer, Confirming the Practicality of the Undertaking.* Appended to it were letters between President Cooke and Captain Beach, in one of which Beach wrote: "Indeed, sir, taking every view of the subject, I see no reason for an unfavorable suspicion towards the Canajoharie & Catskill Railroad. . . ."[5] This reassurance would seem to indicate that some observers had doubts of the company's success.

Nevertheless, on October 27, 1831, a grand procession of dignitaries, including President Cooke for the company and President Day of the Tanner's Bank strode through the streets of Catskill to break ground for the new railroad. A thirteen-gun salute was fired at sunrise, martial music was played, church bells were rung and orations were delivered.[6] Indeed, so many units were included in the marching order that there could not have been a very large crowd lining the streets. After this flamboyant beginning, the company opened its books to stock subscribers, formed several committees and passed numerous resolutions. It did not, however, build a railroad.

The pause resulted from the speculative behavior of investors at this period of American history. Much railroad stock fell into the hands of men unable or unwilling to answer the company's requests for payment, but eager to accept a quick profit.[7] The phenomenon was not confined to railroads, of course, and real estate enjoyed a boom so alarming that Governor Marcy spoke out against imprudence:

> The vacant lands in and about several of our cities and villages have risen, in many instances, several hundred per cent, and large quantities of them have been sold at prices which seem to me to have been produced more by the competition of speculation, rather than any real demand resulting from the increase of our population and general prosperity.[8]

Despite this and other warnings, the railroad promoters formed the Catskill Land Association and proceeded to buy up property along the railroad's projected right-of-way. The group eventually purchased not only farms and homesteads, but seven hundred acres of "mountain land" from which the railroad later purchased timber for bridges and superstructure.[9]

In the years intervening between 1831 and 1835, Catskill villagers were becoming impatient. Having been told of the railroad's glorious prospects, they resented this shameless abandonment of the project. Their commentary on the lack of progress was described by an eye-witness who recorded the event in April of 1832:

> . . . the Catskill people had a very great funeral last week on Thursday night they had a coffin made for the purpose of burying the Rail Road they had lamps with (Mottoes) on them, the Tanners Bank and the Catskill Bank phisic and they have given me so much phisic that it has given me the relax and now I am dead and on the coffin was wrote who killed Cock Robin the performance commenced about 10 OClock they went before Judge Cook's House and there broke all the Lamps and then marched up to the place where they celebrated the breaking of the Ground playing the death march and then buried the Coffin and then they thought the road was dead and buried.[10]

The ceremony was premature, of course, but there were those who doubted that the railroad's life could be long. A contractor on the Mohawk & Hudson wrote to a friend:

> I see by the papers that the stock of the Catskill & Canajoharie Rail Road Company is taken up — If this is not a wild speculation I am much mistaken as it is my opinion that the Mohawk river might more easily be turned out of its valley than to divert the western travel from the same valley — [11]

But there were many who held the opposite view. In New York City, investors were buying up the stock at $95 a share (par value was $50).[12]

When, in 1835, the project was renewed under local auspices, those directors who had made no payments on the stock were removed from office and replaced. At the head of the company was Cooke, with fellow Catskillians John Adams, Amos Cornwall, John M. Donnelly, Jacob Platt and Peter T. Mesick. Others included were John Mason, New York City; Henry Lieber, Canajoharie; and Abijah Mann, Jr., Schoharie.[13] These men at once determined to put the construction work under contract. The man selected to undertake the job was Ephraim Beach, whose enthusiasm was evident and whose credentials were excellent. He offered to complete the undertaking, exclusive of iron, for $550,000.[14]

Ephraim Beach had served in the War of 1812 as a Captain of a company of volunteers and had been promoted to Brevet-Major at the time of discharge. For some time he had been assistant engineer on the Erie Canal, he had surveyed and built the Morris Canal in New Jersey, he had drawn the plans for the Bergen Cut on the Pennsylvania Railroad and he planned and built the Morris & Essex Railroad. This was the man who accepted the post of Chief Engineer for the railroad and who contracted for its construction.[15]

His arrival in Catskill coincided with an intensified drive to improve the economic condition of the village and its Greene County neighbors. The Catskill Land Association, already noted, had been formed by Cooke and others associated with the railroad, including Chief Engineer Beach. Their purpose was to purchase land along and near the proposed right-of-way of the Canajoharie & Catskill Rail Road.[16]

The list of booster organizations grew longer when the Catskill Association (not to be confused with either the Catskill Mountain Association or the Catskill Land Association) sprang to life in December of 1836. This aggregation wished to promote the railroad, as might be expected, but in addition tried to encourage *canal* construction parallel to it! The report of this association issued early the next year complained that since the opening of the Erie Canal, Catskill residents had been "compelled to depend upon a limited business," but that the railroad would "start [the town] forward on a new career with every prospect of outstripping all competition." As for the canal, its route was "pointed out by nature, and [Catskill] should have been originally selected for the termination of the Erie Canal." Thomas B. Cooke, chairman of the Association's Internal Improvement Committee, initiated a petition to the State Legislature in order to have State financial support for these transportation facilities.[17]

Meanwhile, out on the line with rod, transit and chain, Beach and his men were determining, finally, the exact route for the railroad. As his first assistant, Beach had Lewis Germain, who directed both surveys and construction when Major Beach was out of town on other engineering projects. One serious difficulty appeared immediately; a bed of quicksand between the Lime Kiln and Henry M. Vedder's dictated a new line up a long grade, 80 feet to the mile, the steepest slope upon the railroad. Another difficulty was solved, however, when Beach achieved the complete elimination of inclined planes by a careful examination of previously-overlooked territory adjacent to the survey lines.[18]

The roadbed itself would be unballasted, graded earth upon which were laid hemlock ground timbers five by six inches lengthwise. Upon these, cross-ties seven-and-a-half feet long were placed and the support timbers (or wooden rails) of yellow pine were then spiked down. The gauge was standard, that is, four feet eight-and-a-half inches. The iron strap (or rail), which Beach was not obliged to supply, was two-and-a-half inches in width and five-eighths of an inch in thickness.[19] In order to follow a reasonably level and straight pathway, the chief engineer found it necessary to cross the Catskill from one side to the other frequently. Eventually, seven bridges of some length were thrown across the creek and many more of lesser span were erected over its smaller tributaries.[20]

As soon as the right-of-way had been settled upon, Beach let subcontracts to others, often farmers whose land was crossed by the railroad. By the spring of 1837, large piles of English rolled iron for the strap rails were to be seen on Catskill docks, local sawmills were delivering timber to points along the line and grading was well under way. Cooke, in accordance with the contract, had purchased 650 tons of English rail, plates and fixtures for the railroad. Domestic hammered iron was more expensive and in short supply.[21]

Action at last!

CHAPTER THREE

Out on the Line

WHEN Ephraim Beach accepted the construction contract in May of 1836, he expected prompt and full payment for work done by his subcontractors. Neither he nor the company could have foreseen the economic disaster now known as the Panic of 1837. The directors learned that holders of the stock could not respond to calls for payment, so that, in Beach's own words, from paying him "tolerably well," the company "became embarrassed and the work was persevered in, much to the disadvantage of the contractor."[1] Money was badly needed, but even an appeal for a state loan in the amount of $400,000 (ostensibly to make the line double-track rather than single-track) was turned down, though the company was allowed to increase its capital stock from $600,000 to $1,000,000. In their testimony before the Committee on Railroads, the directors alluded to the pressures of "present exigencies."[2] They were saying politely that they could not pay their bills.

In spite of this, out on the line, teams of horses and yokes of oxen were rough grading the right-of-way, stone workers were laying up bridge abutments and local sawmills were buzzing out sills, ties and rails for the superstructure. The property acquired for construction had in many instances been freely given to the company, although there were some stubborn individuals who were not cooperative. One local story is that the Van Vechtens moved the survey stakes so often that the railroad finally accepted their route across this historic farm. Even so, the route came so close to the foundation of the old stone house (reputed to have been built in 1690) that the foundation was nearly undermined. The front entrance became useless with a railroad under the porch, so

the rear of the house became the front, and has remained so to this day.[3] And the work went on.

At a time when almost all public and private improvements in New York were either temporarily abandoned or cut back, the Canajoharie & Catskill Rail Road project, after a brief suspension, resumed with a full work force. The 1837 act which enabled the village of Catskill to subscribe to $100,000 worth of stock was certainly a badly-needed boost.[4]

By January 1, 1838, Major Beach estimated that almost $200,000 had been spent for grading, bridges, ties, surveys, six miles of superstructure (exclusive of iron plates), one passenger and two transportation cars.[5] These three pieces of rolling stock were undoubtedly of local manufacture, although no records exist of their origin. Later in the year, Smith Ward Bullock of the Phoenix Foundry supplied the railroad with four more freight cars and a "controller" (probably a braking device), Fowler Ray installed his patented overload springs on them and Peter Renolds carpentered their upper bodies.[6] Thus, the transportation enterprise enjoyed local support and employed local skills.

In order to expedite the construction work, Beach divided the road into divisions, each to be managed by an assistant engineer. In June of 1838, he hired 20-year-old George Hammell Cook of Chatham, New Jersey, to serve as his assistant on the second division, with headquarters at Oak Hill. Cook had been employed by Beach on the Morris & Essex Railroad in 1836 and 1837 and eventually went on to become head of Rensselaer Institute at Troy and State Geologist for New Jersey.[7] Cook left an account of his service on the Canajoharie & Catskill during 1838, as well as preserving many

The Van Vechten House. Surveyors for the railroad put the line so close to the historic Van Vechten House (1690) that the structure was nearly undermined. This later photo shows the right-of-way of the Catskill Mountain Railway, which followed the C.&C. grade here. *(Collection of Barbara Rivette)*

letters from friends who stayed on during 1839 and 1840.

Young Cook arrived in Albany on the *Swallow*, the steamboat fated to die a fiery death some years later, and took the stage for Catskill. There he was met by his immediate superior, Lewis Germain, and by Elihu Cotes and J. B. Bassinger. He immediately set out to inspect the work and stepped into a railroad coach bound for South Cairo, where he changed to a stage for Oak Hill. His job had begun.[8]

One of the first official communications Cook received after his arrival in the village of Oak Hill was this letter from the railroad office in Catskill:

To G. H. Cook, Assistant in Charge 2nd Division
Oak Hill, N. Y.
June 28, 1838

To the Assistants & field men
of the Engineering department
of the Canajoharie & Catskill
Railroad
Gentm

with your approval the following regulations will be observed in future by the Corps.

1st Precedence will be given to superiors in rank.

2nd In rank the following is the order 1st Chief Engineer 2d Assistant 3d Assistant in Charge 4th Rodman 5th Chainman and Axman.

3d When the Chief Engineer is addressed the head will be uncovered unless walking in company in the field.

4th No gentlemen will take his seat at table until those superior in rank are seated & seats will be taken in order of rank.

5th No gentleman will appropriate to himself a bed or sleeping apartment until those of higher rank have made choice of those they wish to occupy.

6th All proper orders given by a superior will be promptly obeyed without discussion or words if understood.

7th When a superior in rank is giving orders to contractors or others he will not without leave be interrupted nor will anyone excepting the Assistant in charge give orders of instructions to contractors in presence of a superior in rank.

8th Any wanton neglect of duty or intentional violation of the orders will be reported as a complaint against the person as doing to the Chief Engineer.

With respect I am yours
L. J. Germain I Asst.

The homely discipline embodied here reflects the military ancestry of civil engineering and the military background of the early engineers (Major Beach, Captain McNeill, Lieutenant Pickell, Colonel Perrault, etc.)

By July 4th, subcontractors were grubbing, scraping, blasting and raising much dust. Later in the same month, Cook reported that the weather had been "dry so long that a stake will hardly go into the ground." But there were ways to keep cool, as he noted on July 14, 1838:

> After tea went in bathing and after we had got out met some ladies who were coming up to meet us. Just escaped. Retired at ten.

Two days later he saw a large collection of schoolboys bathing with their teacher. And on the next Sunday, he picked three quarts of raspberries.[9]

The heat was not the only unpleasant element to be endured by Cook and his surveyors:

> I set the instrument in front of Mr. Patrey's house and the old gentleman sat at the window and made the Dr. [Doctor Hulbert, whose presence on the survey crew is never explained] look out how he took stakes out of the fence. He talked to me about the injustice which the R. R. Company wished to do him and said that they should not commence work until the damage was settled

and that it was a mere favor letting us come on to lay out the work.[10]

The dispute was eventually settled by Cooke and Beach and the work proceeded. By September 15th, Schurff's abutment had been completed and the workmen, all "Dutchmen" (either Hollanders or Germans, for the distinction was often blurred) held an impromptu celebration:

> As soon as they had got the work done they commenced singing and sung several songs after which the whiskey jug was circulated and then one of them got up on a pole to which the tackle was rigged and after taking another drink of whiskey and then made some sort of an address and returned thanks to the Almighty for his care over them during their work, he then got down onto the wall again and took another drink of the whiskey after which they all joined in singing another song or two when they went home. During the address they all paid the strictest attention and a boy who forgot to take off his hat had it knocked off very unceremoniously.[11]

By the end of 1838, $303,808.20 had been spent on the railroad and a "locomotive steam engine" had been ordered. According to the Chief Engineer, grading and superstructure on the first 26 miles was substantially complete. Although these were the most difficult and expensive miles on the entire route, fifteen miles were in use with horse power and the other eleven nearly ready for laying of iron.[12] In view of the financial paralysis gripping the country, the achievement was remark-

Rock Cut near Winansville. Drill marks in the rock here are enduring evidence of the tedious and dangerous work undertaken by construction crews. When these holes were filled with black powder and ignited, the explosive force blasted large chunks of rock out of the hillside, making a level roadbed possible. (*Photograph by the author*)

23

C. & C. Superstructure. These mementoes in the Durham Center Museum are in remarkably good condition for their age. Spike holes in the wooden stringer are 15 inches from center to center, but the strap iron is not drilled to correspond. The mystery is soluble, however, for a large supply of English strap iron was stored for use beyond Cooksburgh. This piece undoubtedly came from the unused portion. *(Photograph by the author)*

Culvert between Oak Hill and Winansville. Still standing and serviceable is this little culvert west of Winansville. The entire structure is dry-laid (without mortar) as were all masonry projects on the railroad. Note the skillfully fitted *voussoirs* in the arch. *(Photograph by the author)*

able. Fortunately, the company had found a financial backer.

This backer was the government of New York State which, in Chapter 240 of the Laws of 1838, agreed to match funds with the company's expenditures. The act, as it operated, issued "Canajoharie & Catskill Rail Road State Stock" in the amount of $100,000 when the railroad had spent an equal sum. As written, however, the act specified a different ratio, that is, the company had to spend $150,000 for each $100,000 in aid. Somewhere between the Legislature's action and the printing of the bill, the figures were changed, or rather, not changed to reflect an amendment containing the 1.50 to 1.00 ratio. Subsequent discovery of the error led to a lengthy investigation into the affairs of the railroad company. Fraud was suspected on the part of the officers, but the charge was not proved. All that could be shown was that the company had probably obtained $50,000 without equal security in railroad construction.[13]

Misfortune followed on misfortune, for the winter of 1838-1839 brought a destructive flood to the railroad. Lewis Germain, Beach's first assistant, recorded bridge abutments swept away, bridges knocked down, embankments undermined and minor damage everywhere. He estimated that reconstruction would cost $10,000. The company, unwisely, chose to suppress any news of the catastrophe. But anyone who inspected the line could see that substantial repair was needed. Because the company refused to release its own estimate of damage, the public suspected the worst. According to Germain, public estimates of the loss ranged from a conservative $25,000 to a hysterical $100,000.[14]

Nevertheless, the future of the Canajoharie & Catskill was clouded. Citizens and subcontractors had petitioned the legislature to make the investigation, an ominous sign. Local support for the railroad seemed to be disintegrating.

At Canajoharie, too, confidence was lacking, as this comment published in the *Catskill Messenger* testifies:

> It has always been a question whether Canajoharie would receive much advantage from it. Our resources are abundant, and the facilities for getting to market have answered our demands, but if others, *seeing our prosperity*, wish to open communications with us, we wish them to prose-

George Hammell Cook, Assistant Engineer. Young Cook learned about engineering the hard way, first on the Morris & Essex and then on the C. & C. His personal papers provide a first-hand account of the C. & C.'s construction. This is a later photograph taken when he had entered academic life. *(Archives of Rutgers, The State University)*

cute the work and let us know, unequivocally, what their intentions are.[15]

And in the wake of the furor over the railroad's trouble in the State Legislature, the *Catskill Recorder* on May 30, 1839, insisted that "all operations upon the railroad should be now and forever suspended." For the railroad was rapidly becoming a political issue, and a cause of quarrels between men. Ephraim Beach's son Zenas wrote his friend Cook that "the private characters of the most respectable men of the town have been libelled over & over again."[16]

The two local newspapers split on the project, with this representative comment appearing in the pro-railroad *Messenger:*

> The interests of this section of the country, and especially the prosperity of this village, have been hitherto, and bid fair to continue to be, sacrificed, to gratify private animosity and personal vindictiveness. We venture to affirm, (and, if our position is denied, to demonstrate) that had it not been for this cause, the Canajoharie and Catskill Railroad would long ago [have] been in successful operation.[17]

Although the repairs were effected and the investigation was completed, the events of the preceding months had cast a pall of gloom over the entire enterprise.

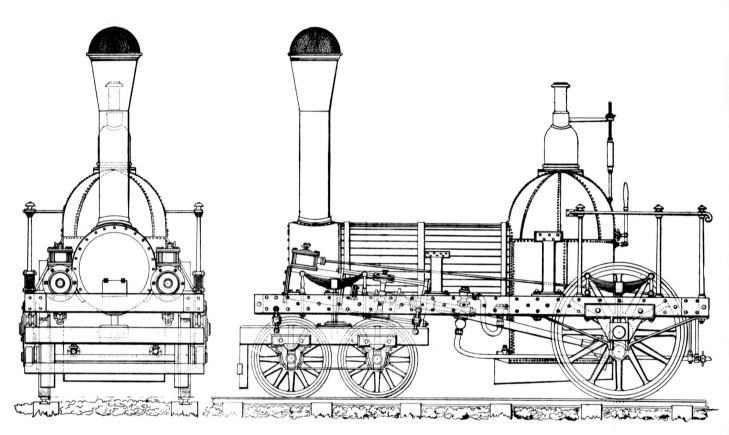

LOCOMOTIVE ENGINE

MANUFACTURED BY H.R. DUNHAM & CO.

N.Y.

FRONT ELEVATION

SIDE ELEVATION

Locomotive Engine Manufactured by H. R. Dunham & Co., N. Y. P. R. Hodge produced this lithograph for his book, *The Steam Engine*, in 1840. Since Dunham probably built no more than 10 4-2-0's, this drawing is undoubtedly an accurate representation of locomotives of that wheel arrangement, including the C.&C.'s engine. *(Photograph courtesy of the Smithsonian Institution)*

CHAPTER FOUR

Smoke on the Horizon

"THE locomotive has not made its appearance in this neighborhood as yet but is expected up next week — and candidly believe it will be up without fail . . ." wrote J. B. Bassinger from Winansville (East Durham) to his friend Cook, who had taken a teaching position in Chatham, New Jersey. The date was November 6, 1839. Despite the young engineer's optimism, weeks of autumnal splendor passed and still no smoke appeared on the horizon, months of bleak winter struck the little hamlet and the steam cars did not venture up the valley of the Catskill. Not until spring weather had softened the harsh mountain snows did the snorting iron horse nose its way up the steep grades to Winansville. It had been a long and hard struggle, not only for the train of cars, but for the railroad as well.

Another man who had unbounding enthusiasm for the railroad was Lewis J. Germain, Beach's assistant at the Catskill office. Even though he had seen angry subcontractors march into the office demanding their money, despite his own threat to quit in an earlier dispute with the Major and regardless of petty annoyances like his son practicing dancing lessons in the office (which confused and annoyed Bassinger), L. J. Germain never lost faith in himself or the project.[1] Particularly pleasing to him was the reception accorded his new invention, a six-wheeled railroad passenger car. The prototype stood just outside his window, on Canajoharie & Catskill rails. Patented on May 7, 1839 (U. S. Patent 1,145), the running gear was its distinctive feature. Three separate truck units, the first and third pinned at the center to the car body and the middle frame independent of the body, made up the car's underpinnings. The center unit turned with the end frames through a rack and segment wheel on one side and a double cross

joint on the other. In this way, Germain believed that sharp curves could more easily and more safely be negotiated. Where bends were frequent and severe, as on both the Canajoharie & Catskill and the Hudson & Berkshire, this was no small consideration.

No record survives of the use of the six-wheeled car on the Canajoharie & Catskill, but its inventor and promoter shipped it to Hudson, N. Y. for a mid-winter demonstration on the Hudson & Berkshire:

On Thursday I went up to Hudson — and rode on their road — and such a time as we had — hey day — I am in doubt yet — whether or no I am in bounds — we went out to the state line — they not having been out before in a long time — the track was well covered with snow and . . . glassy with ice (of which they have about as much as we) digging and scraping was the order of the day — we ran off the track twice — full tilt — and I can assure you if you have not tried it — that there is not so much sport in bouncing over the ties down hill — and if we had not found ties and sills piled along the Road — we might have been there yet as it was we found it no Fools job to get a fourteen ton engine back on the track — we were nearly three howers at one time boosting the "old steam waggon." They have got a pretty decent sort of a Rail Road but it is as crooked as a rams horn . . .[2]

Apparently the car also performed well on Germain's home road, for he reported to Cook that Judge Cooke and Major Beach praised it highly.[3]

The company's own ten freight cars were hauled by horses through most, and perhaps all, of 1839. The completed line extended to Winansville by the end of the year and regular teaming trips were made to that point. The locomotive arrived from New York City at some time late in 1839, unnoticed by the local newspapers. This silence about the strange importation can be explained, probably, by the intense political controversy between Whigs and Democrats, which the

27

Dunham's Iron Foundry and Locomotive Engine Works. Edward W. Clay's watercolor drawing titled *North River Iron Foundry* shows the birthplace of the C.&C.'s MOUNTAINEER, one of about 20 little engines built by Dunham between 1836 and 1839. (*Edward W. C. Arnold Collection. Loaned by the Metropolitan Museum of Art. Photograph courtesy of the Museum of the City of New York*)

---

local partisan press reported in great detail and at great length.

The new motive power may have given trouble at the start of its service. Beers' history of 1884 states flatly that the locomotive was "a failure" and that "the old stage horse" replaced it.[4] Undoubtedly, there could have been initial difficulties, for the state of the art of locomotive building was not far advanced. The manufacturer, H. R. Dunham & Co., had had little experience in the business; indeed, the firm seems to have entered the field only briefly (1836-1839) and then to have withdrawn completely. Whatever the difficulties, evidence exists that the locomotive was in regular service during 1840 and 1841, and until the railroad failed in 1842. Light in weight (9¼ tons) and low in power (a single pair of high drivers), the Canajoharie & Catskill's MOUNTAINEER was a $6,300 investment. Its imperfections are now recognized, but were not in 1839. The Dunham engines had tall blast pipes (exhausting used cylinder steam high in the smoke box) which created a draft principally on the upper boiler tubes. This in turn allowed a pile-up of ash and cinders at the bottom of the smokebox, further reducing the draft. Thus, the engine would not steam efficiently.[5] Nevertheless, it could move a train of cars, and did, frequently. It sometimes needed aid in starting, but it ran.

When a sufficient head of steam had been built, engineer James Eckler would haul back on the throttle and the engine would inch forward. If the day's lading was heavy, the locomotive might stall or spin its wheels, and a stand-by team of horses would amble up to the pilot beam and hook on.[6] With this added pull, the train would snuffle along Water Street toward the first bridge across the Catskill. Here the momentum of the rolling cars

28

Barrel car in use about 1837. These B.&O. rail wagons correspond to John Baldwin's description of Canajoharie & Catskill freight cars and resemble strongly the four-wheeled carriages trailing the train in Thomas Cole's painting. Crude link and pin couplers connect the cars. (*Baltimore & Ohio Railroad*)

would allow, and the proximity of the narrow span would require, the unhitching of the team. Once over the bridge, the steep grade lay behind and three miles of undulating track lay ahead.

The end of the line in late 1839 was Winansville, where J. B. Bassinger waited so expectantly for the MOUNTAINEER. In November horses hauled up cars of iron and brick for the Oak Hill foundry and hay for White's hay press.[7] The extension of the road by Major Beach had been renegotiated with Treasurer Peter T. Mesick, who insisted upon a lower figure than had previously been agreed to. The contractor was obliged to lay track to Oak Hill or Benjamin's during the winter and to Potter's Hollow when the company could supply the needed money. Beach claimed that he lost money on the original 26-mile contract and stood to lose even more on the revised arrangement.[8] But he undertook the work.

Finally, on March 19, 1840, the *Catskill Messenger* carried this announcement:

> The Rail-Road — The Locomotive MOUNTAINEER commenced her regular trips on Monday last, upon the Canajoharie Road, running out as far as Stevens' in Durham.

At about this time, a young boy looked in awe at this wonderful new machine:

> When I was a little shaver of about eleven years, my father took me with him one day down below South Cairo, on business. It was rather late in the fall and we drove down near a large mill that stood on the Catskill Creek about three miles west of Leeds.

> By and by we came to a place where there was a queer looking machine with what appeared to me a frightful looking chimney and a big stove on wheels, which stood directly across the highway. My father said: "Johnny, that is the new railroad and that is the Indian," as I understood him, but, of course, he must have said "engine."

29

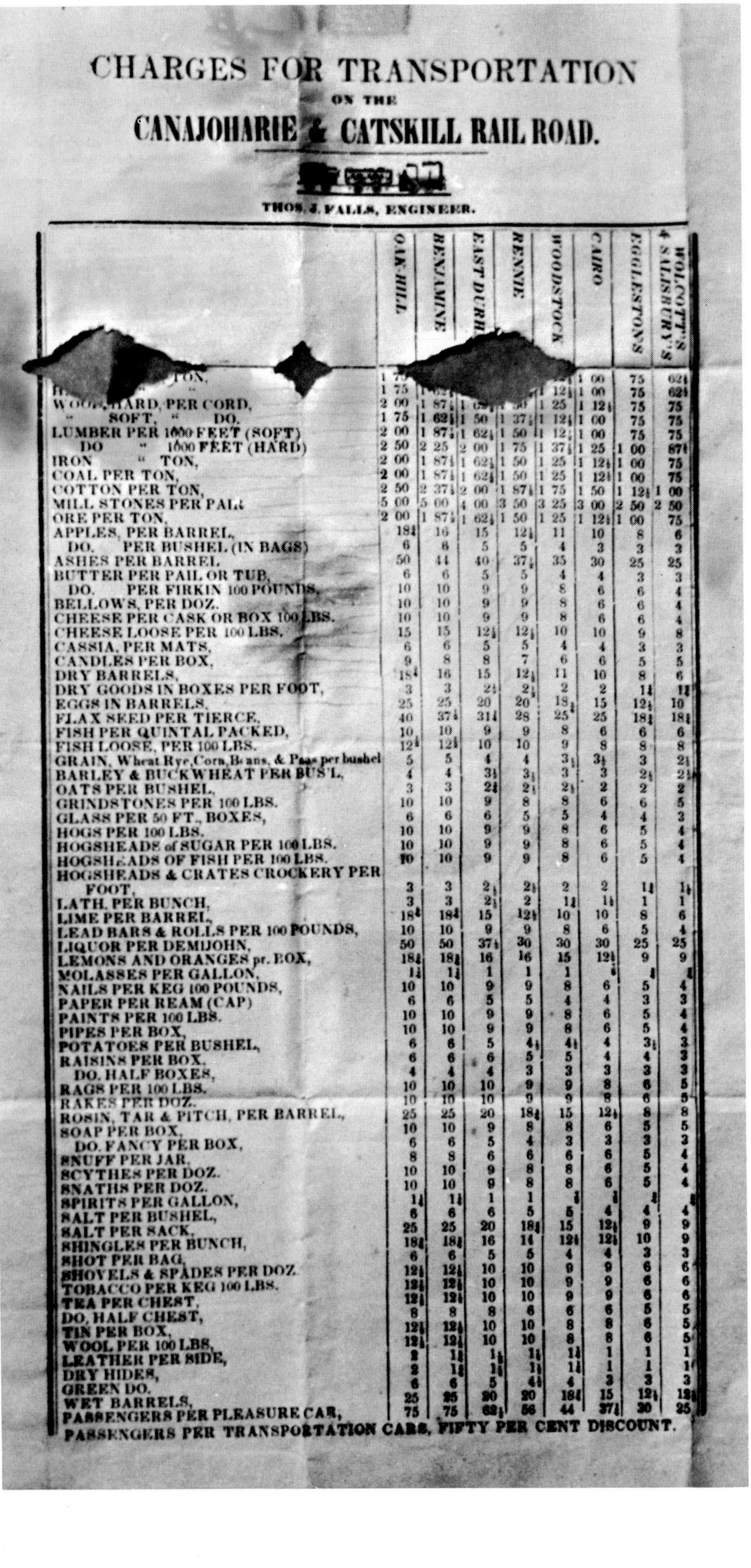

CHARGES FOR TRANSPORTATION
ON THE
CANAJOHARIE & CATSKILL RAIL ROAD.

THOS. J. FALLS, ENGINEER.

	OAK-HILL	BENJAMINE	EAST-DURHAM	RENNE	WOODSTOCK	CAIRO	EGGLESTONS	WOLCOTT'S & SALISBURY'S
.... TON,	1 7...					1 00	75	62½
W... HARD, PER CORD,	2 00	1 87½			12½ 1 00	75	62½	
" SOFT, " DO.	1 75	1 62½	1 50	1 37½	1 25 1 12½	1 00	75	75
LUMBER PER 1000 FEET (SOFT)	2 00	1 87½	1 62½	1 50	12½ 1 00	75	75	
DO " 1000 FEET (HARD)	2 50	2 25	2 00	1 75	1 37½ 1 25	1 00	87½	
IRON " TON,	2 00	1 87½	1 62½	1 50	1 25 1 12½	1 00	75	
COAL PER TON,	2 00	1 87½	1 62½	1 50	1 25 1 12½	1 00	75	
COTTON PER TON,	2 50	2 37½	2 00	1 87½	1 75 1 50	1 12½	1 00	
MILL STONES PER PAIR	5 00	5 00	4 00	3 50	3 25 3 00	2 50	2 50	
ORE PER TON,	2 00	1 87½	1 62½	1 50	1 25 1 12½	1 00	75	
APPLES, PER BARREL,	18½	16	15	12½	11	10	8	6
DO. PER BUSHEL (IN BAGS)	6	6	5	5	4	3	3	3
ASHES PER BARREL	50	44	40	37½	35	30	25	25
BUTTER PER PAIL OR TUB,	6	6	5	5	4	4	3	3
DO. PER FIRKIN 100 POUNDS,	10	10	9	9	8	6	6	4
BELLOWS, PER DOZ.	10	10	9	9	8	6	6	4
CHEESE PER CASK OR BOX 100 LBS.	10	10	9	9	8	6	6	4
CHEESE LOOSE PER 100 LBS.	15	15	12½	12½	10	10	9	8
CASSIA, PER MATS,	6	6	5	5	4	4	3	3
CANDLES PER BOX,	9	8	8	7	6	6	5	5
DRY BARRELS,	18½	16	15	12½	11	10	8	6
DRY GOODS IN BOXES PER FOOT,	3	3	2½	2½	2	2	1½	1½
EGGS IN BARRELS,	25	25	20	20	18½	15	12½	10
FLAX SEED PER TIERCE,	40	37½	31½	28	25	25	18½	18½
FISH PER QUINTAL PACKED,	10	10	9	9	8	6	6	6
FISH LOOSE, PER 100 LBS.	12½	12½	10	10	9	8	8	8
GRAIN, Wheat Rye,Corn,Beans, & Peas per bushel	5	5	4	4	3½	3½	3	2½
BARLEY & BUCKWHEAT PER BUS'L,	4	4	3½	3½	3	3	2½	2½
OATS PER BUSHEL,	3	3	2½	2½	2½	2	2	2
GRINDSTONES PER 100 LBS.	10	10	9	8	8	6	6	5
GLASS PER 50 FT., BOXES,	6	6	6	5	5	4	4	3
HOGS PER 100 LBS.	10	10	9	9	8	6	5	4
HOGSHEADS of SUGAR PER 100 LBS.	10	10	9	9	8	6	5	4
HOGSHEADS OF FISH PER 100 LBS.	10	10	9	9	8	6	5	4
HOGSHEADS & CRATES CROCKERY PER FOOT,	3	3	2½	2½	2	2	1½	1½
LATH, PER BUNCH,	3	3	2½	2½	2	1½	1	1
LIME PER BARREL,	18½	18½	15	12½	10	10	8	6
LEAD BARS & ROLLS PER 100 POUNDS,	10	10	9	9	8	6	5	4
LIQUOR PER DEMIJOHN,	50	50	37½	30	30	30	25	25
LEMONS AND ORANGES pr. BOX,	18½	18½	16	16	15	12½	9	9
MOLASSES PER GALLON,	1½	1½	1	1	1		½	½
NAILS PER KEG 100 POUNDS,	10	10	9	9	8	6	5	4
PAPER PER REAM (CAP)	6	6	5	5	4	4	3	3
PAINTS PER 100 LBS.	10	10	9	9	8	6	5	4
PIPES PER BOX,	10	10	9	9	8	6	5	4
POTATOES PER BUSHEL,	6	6	5	4½	4½	4	3½	3
RAISINS PER BOX,	4	4	6	5	5	4	3	3
DO. HALF BOXES,	4	4	4	3	3	3	3	3
RAGS PER 100 LBS.	10	10	10	9	9	8	6	5
RAKES PER DOZ.	10	10	10	9	8	8	6	5
ROSIN, TAR & PITCH, PER BARREL,	25	25	20	18½	15	12½	8	8
SOAP PER BOX,	10	10	9	8	8	6	5	5
DO. FANCY PER BOX,	6	6	5	4	3	3	3	3
SNUFF PER JAR,	8	8	6	6	6	6	5	4
SCYTHES PER DOZ.	10	10	9	8	8	6	5	4
SNATHS PER DOZ.	10	10	9	8	8	6	5	4
SPIRITS PER GALLON,	1½	1½	1	1	1		½	½
SALT PER BUSHEL,	6	6	6	5	5	4	4	4
SALT PER SACK,	25	25	20	18½	15	12½	9	9
SHINGLES PER BUNCH,	18½	18½	16	14	12½	12½	10	9
SHOT PER BAG,	6	6	5	5	4	4	3	3
SHOVELS & SPADES PER DOZ.	12½	12½	10	10	9	9	6	6
TOBACCO PER KEG 100 LBS.	12½	12½	10	10	9	9	6	6
TEA PER CHEST,	12½	12½	10	10	9	9	6	6
DO. HALF CHEST,	8	8	8	6	6	6	5	5
TIN PER BOX,	12½	12½	10	10	8	8	6	5
WOOL PER 100 LBS.	12½	12½	10	10	8	8	6	5
LEATHER PER SIDE,	2	1½	1½		1½	1½	1	1
DRY HIDES,	2	1½	1½	1½	1½	1	1	1
GREEN DO.	6	6	5	4½	4	3	3	3
WET BARRELS,	25	25	20	20	18½	15	12½	12½
PASSENGERS PER PLEASURE CAR,	75	75	62½	56	44	37½	30	25

PASSENGERS PER TRANSPORTATION CARS, FIFTY PER CENT DISCOUNT.

Charges for Transportation on the Canajoharie & Catskill Rail Road. Here is a delightful picture of early nineteenth century life — liquor per demijohn, bellows per dozen, candles per box, butter per tub, hogsheads of fish, millstones per pair, snuff per jar, etc. Passengers in the "pleasure car" paid about three cents a mile; those roughing it among the barrels and bags and hides paid half that. *(Photograph by the author)*

I was rather skittish yet curious, and our steady old horse was more so than I was, and began to rear so that father had to get out and hold him by the head. Then I had time to look closely at the "Indian." It had a tall, rather tapering smoke stack about seven feet high. There was no cab, I remember, for later on when cabs were adopted, I noticed the difference. There was a tender next to the engine, a short four wheeled affair. There was a single pair of drivers about three feet in diameter, and while the affair would look very small and insignificant to-day, it seemed to me then, as big as a barn would now. The engine and the tender were not more than twelve feet in length, but the brass bell that was on the engine, that they kept ringing, took my eye, and I thought it sounded very pretty. There were three short four-wheeled freight cars that resembled the ore and coal cars of the present day [1897], and in the rear of these were two passenger cars that were simply four-wheeled platform cars with old stage coach bodies thereon and fastened with bolts. In each of the cars were perhaps a half dozen passengers, and I, boylike, wondered how they dared to risk their lives in that way. By and by, after the track, which was composed of bar iron about two inches across and half an inch [thick] bolted on string pieces, was repaired, which occupied a few minutes, the bell rang and the engine, slowly at first and then with increasing speed, moved off up the road.

I was told it went to Durham and that the cars did not go any further.[9]

Extension beyond Durham met opposition in the person of Henry Hedges, who finally but reluctantly accepted the intrusion onto his lands of the MOUNTAINEER and "brigade" of cars. Submitted to arbitration, Hedges was awarded $500 in damages on November 26, 1840.[10]

By April of 1840 the tracklayers had spiked down the strap iron onto the wooden rail as far as Oak Hill and regular daily service began. A part of this service was for the political congregations so much a part of the life of the new nation, as reported in the *Messenger* for April 23, 1840:

> Whig Convention at Cairo — The delegation from this place was quite large — the number of those who went out upon the cars amounting to *ninety-five;* the train consisted of some seven or eight cars, upon the largest of which our "Corn Bread and Hard Cider Boys" had erected a *"Log Cabin"* which was furnished with a barrel of *"hard cider,"* a loaf of "corn bread" of monstrous dimensions, a roast pig, rice puddings, crackers and cheese, & c., & c.

These overloaded and victual-garnished cars bound for Cairo must have provided a true test of the pulling power of the MOUNTAINEER. One

wonders if the dining car patrons lasted through their ordeal as well.

When the locomotive and train entered the village of Oak Hill for the first time, they rumbled over three newly-built bridges, all of lattice construction, en route. These spans were light, simple and, more important to the railroad, economical. The daily round trips continued until Monday, May 4th, when the westbound train rolled onto the second bridge, under the shadow of High Rock. The waters still washed high and strong on the wooden center piers, though a torrential spring freshet had abated somewhat. Nevertheless, the center of the bridge sagged and fell under the weight of the cars, to the discordant sound of snapping timbers. Three freight cars and two passenger cars with about forty persons aboard dropped into the flood. Jehiel Tyler of Durham was killed, an unidentified colored man suffered the fracture of a leg and both thighs and several others were less seriously injured.[11]

The engine crew escaped harm, for the MOUNTAINEER had reached the western bank just as the span fell. Merchandise, people and bridge debris were swept downstream by the cold waters, in a wreck scene which must have been a terrifying one.[12]

Stunned as it was by this newest misfortune, the company immediately contracted with Major Beach for reconstruction of the bridge. For its economic life depended not only upon the considerable freight traffic beyond the bridge, in the Oak Hill area, but upon the recovery of the locomotive from its solitary location at the far end of the line. By June 4th, the contractor had erected a new brace bridge at a cost of almost $10,000. When Beach claimed this amount, however, the railroad officials refused to pay and the major noted that he was "thus compelled to give up a large, a large and just demand to avoid a *vexatious litigation with a swindling company.*" Lest the blame (and thus the expense) be laid to him, Beach noted that there had been heavy rains that spring and that the lattice bridge had been expressly ordered by the company instead of a planned heavier structure.[13]

When the railroad resumed normal operation on June 5th, the little train puffed along the strap-iron rails from the Railroad Office to the station

Wreck site at High Rock. In 1840 a Town lattice bridge extended from half way down the cliff at the right to a point hidden in the branches at the left. Here the train crashed through the bridge floor to the creek bed below. (*Photograph by the author*)

Roadbed at High Rock, looking east. From this ledge in the center of the photo, where the tall hemlock now stands, the train rattled onto the High Rock bridge, whose supports had been weakened by flood water. (*Photograph by the author*)

just north of Cairo and on to Oak Hill. The rebuilding of the High Rock trestle as a braced bridge delayed completion of the construction to Cooksburg, but, true to his commitment, Chief Engineer Beach pushed the line as far as the road to Potter's Hollow, 26¼ miles from Catskill and 800 feet above tidewater. This became the end of track and a depot was erected in January or February of 1841,[14] at a point far short of Canajoharie, but close enough to the productive Schoharie Valley to attract neighboring farmers, mill-owners and merchants.

Unfortunately, even though the western terminal sat high above the end of track at Catskill, the locomotive when headed "down" to the Hudson encountered its greatest resistance here. At about three miles below Cooksburg a grade of 58 feet to the mile occurred. Not insuperable in itself, the upward slope came after a series of three reverse curves. At times the laboring engine hammered along at great velocity (perhaps as much as 20 miles per hour), screeched into the three sharp curves, swayed first to one side, then to the other and stopped at the foot of the grade with a shudder.[15] If the engineer could not build up sufficient steam pressure or obtain enough momentum on a second try, it is likely that passenger-power propelled the train over the hill.

Given the Canajoharie & Catskill's nightmarish topography, its tarnished reputation, its fading local support, and its shaky financial basis, the final outcome could be no surprise.

After the fatal accident at High Rock, the Catskill journals gave even less space to the railroad than they had before. Even the railroad's advocate, the *Catskill Messenger*, referred to the company's doubtful position and stated its belief that inadequate public notice was being given to the C. & C. in Albany and New York.[16] Subsequently, these notices about the railroad became scarce and incidental, like this *Messenger* squib of December 31, 1840:

> Better late than never — Some where about two months ago, (when we were wrapt up in politics) we received via the C. & C. Railroad a bag of "*sundries*," such as apples, pears, quinces, stocking yarn, etc. etc., from some one who had the modesty to withhold his or her name.

If it were not for the confirmation found in an old receipt book, the operation of the railroad after

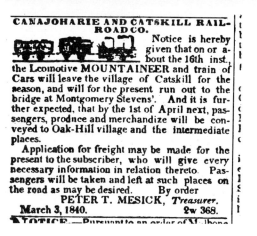

Advertisement for train service. Still not completed in early 1840, the railroad nevertheless offered transportation until a few weeks later when the bridge collapse cut the line, with the locomotive stranded twenty-two miles from Catskill. (*The* Catskill Messenger)

1840 might be in doubt. This record, though incomplete and nearly illegible, shows that daily expenditures for wood, for pumping water, for track repair and for train operation were being paid during 1841 and part of 1842. Here, in fact, can be found the only available information about railroad employees. James Eckler earned $18.47 on May 13, 1841 "for running Engine," and $85.39 "for running Locomotive" on July 31. Fireman William Weed received $38.88 on July 31. Trainmen, who also frequently worked on track maintenance, were Augustus Hamlin, John Cornwall, John P. Goetschius and Richard P. Elmendorf. Giles Sutton, on January 5, 1842, accepted $129.81 "for work in Running Train," a description which differs enough from the notation on the trainmen's receipts ("for work on cars") to indicate that he was the captain or conductor of the C. & C.'s train.[17] Others were certainly employed, but their names are lost to us.

Apparently Ephraim Beach's connection with the railroad ended when he had laid the last wooden rail into Cooksburg (actually the line passed the depot and ran a quarter mile beyond it), but he maintained his Catskill residence for the remainder of his life. His assistant was now J. B. Bassinger, who left town for other employment early in April of 1841.[18] The later career of Germain cannot be ascertained, but he is undoubtedly the gentleman who exhibited a model of a "six-wheeled car" at the Franklin Institute late in 1840.[19] George Hammel Cook had entered the academic life, becoming Senior Professor and head

FINALLY, THE SURVEY OF THAT PORTION OF THE ROAD CONSTRUCTED.

The principal object of this survey was to ascertain the character of the grades and curves, to examine the bridges and superstructure, and the condition of the road generally. The following table exhibits the grades commencing at Cookesburgh the Northerly termination.

TABLE.

Miles	Chains	Direction	Rate per mile (feet)	Elevation above tide (feet)	Locations
				791 6	Begins 26 ch'ns north of Depot.
	60	descent,	46 2	728 0	Road to Potter's Hollow.
	12	"	42 6	751 6	Hand's Tannery.
	26	"	57 5	732 9	
	56	"	41 7	703 7	Brown's Fulling Mill.
1	22	"	40 7	652 2	
	18	level		652 2	Richardson's Mill.
	40	descent,	51 2	626 2	Oak Hill,
	6	"	20 0	624 7	
	22	"	58 2	608 7	
	8	"	43 0	604 4	
	10	"	56 0	597 4	Mr. Stanard's.
	24	"	26 0	589 5	Opposite Tremain's tannery.
	18	"	47 1	578 9	
	6	"	60 0	574 7	
	4	"	44 0	572 2	
	20	level			Bridge over Catskill.
	8	descent,	35 0	569 7	
	6	level			
	8	ascent,	29 0	571 5	
	6	descent,	18 6	570 1	
	27	"	64 0	547 7	Bridge over Catskill.
	23	level			
	62	descent,	57 9	503 3	
	2	level			
	32	ascent,	57 7	526 7	Hedges.
	8	level			
	18	descent,	56 4	514 0	
	26	level			East Durham.
	28	descent,	58 8	493 4	
	46	"	64 2	456 5	Hay Press.
	14	"	42 3	449 1	
	16	level			
	14	descent,	30 3	442 7	
	6	level			
	16	ascent,	43 0	452 0	
	6	level			
	40	ascent,	27 6	465 7	
	26	level			
	8	descent,	57 0	460 4	
	22	"	60 4	443 8	
	28	"	39 5	429 9	{ Bridge 26 ft. span over small stream.
1	10	"	39 0	363 5	
	16	"	18 5	359 8	
	28	"	9 2	356 6	
	12	ascent,	33 3	301 6	
	14	level			Road.

Miles	Chains	Direction	Rate per Mile (feet)	Elevation above tide (feet)	Location
	8	descent,	28 0	358 3	Opposite Woodstock.
	24	level			
	20	descent,	14 8	355 1	
	30	ascent,	20 8	362 9	Samuel Bennett's.
	8	level			
	24	descent,	58 7	345 3	
	10	"	48 8	339 2	Cairo.
	6	level			
	26	ascent,	60 3	358 8	
	12	level			
	18	ascent,	48 9	367 8	
	8	level			
1	50	descent,	59 0	271 9	Rock Excavation.
	78	"	59 2	214 2	Opposite Mr. Blackmar's.
	10	"	60 0	206 7	
	12	ascent,	10 0	205 6	Depot.
	22	descent,	71 3	185 6	South Cairo.
	14	ascent,	19 3	188 8	"Scotch Rock."
	20	descent,	42 8	178 1	
	6	level			
	42	ascent,	10 3	183 5	
	50	level			Wolcott's Mills.
	10	ascent,	39 2	188 4	
	10	"	44 0	199 3	
	14	level			
	6	ascent,	36 0	196 6	
	8	"	40 0	200 6	Toll Gate.
	8	descent,	50 0	195 6	
	20	"	17 6	191 2	
	30	"	55 7	170 3	
	8	level			Henry M. Vedder's.
	16	descent,	80 5	154 2	
	18	"	56 4	148 2	
	26	"	73 1	116 1	Lime Kiln.
	6	"	61 3	111 5	
	14	"	77 7	97 9	Third bridge over the Catskill.
	8	"	28 0	95 1	
	64	"	59 6	47 4	Paper Mill.
	4	"	18 0	46 5	
	12	"	58 0	37 8	
	4	"	22 0	36 7	
	16	level			
	26	descent,	19 0	30 7	
	22	level			
	20	descent,	23 6	24 6	Second bridge over the Catskill.
	18	level .			
	10	ascent,	19 2	27 0	
	12	descent,	10 0	25 5	First " " "
	8	ascent,	1 2	26 7	
	4	descent,	34 0	25 0	
	8	"	79 0	17 1	Rail Road Office.
	6	level			

Brodhead's survey of the completed railroad. This table furnishes accurate information on the road as built, although many locations indicated have disappeared.

Abutment at High Rock, looking west. Almost obscured by summer foliage, the dry-laid stone abutment for the High Rock Bridge still stands, as solid as it was in 1840, when it gave a firm footing to the MOUNTAINEER. *(Photograph by the author)*

of Rensselaer Institute in Troy, N. Y., in 1842. Ambitious men were looking elsewhere for permanent positions.

When the company failed to pay the interest on its $200,000 state railroad stock in 1841, the end was in sight. Canajoharie & Catskill Rail Road, the short-cut to the west, had few friends left.

Of those few, a committee was formed consisting of Ezra Hawley (now the railroad's president), Peter Osterhoudt, Sr. and William C. Bouck, soon to be governor and, significantly, a resident of Schoharie County. Edward Brodhead, a noted civil engineer, was retained for yet another survey of the entire route, the fourth and final survey in the series — Swift's, Pickell's, McNeill's and now Brodhead's. In January of 1842 the report came off the press, and it was, predictably, favorable. Brodhead alluded vaguely to criticism of the route selected by Beach, particularly the short radius of the curve at the bridge near Leeds. He was unable to improve this location and considered the leveling of the Cooksburg-to-East Durham grade the only practical modification necessary on the completed line.

An appended letter from the committee pleaded for public support in order to extend the rails at least to the Schoharie Valley, 15 miles distant. There, they said, it would tap rich agricultural resources and fill not only railroad cars but railroad coffers.[20]

The dream of long trains and tidy profits soon dissipated. The MOUNTAINEER was to steam along the upper reaches of the Catskill no more. The surveys and plans would become historical curiosities. The Catskill terminal building would never rise on the waterfront. The railroad was dying.

On May 20, 1842, the Canajoharie & Catskill was sold by the State of New York to Amos Cornwall and associates for $11,600.[21] The rails were torn up and the equipment dispersed. The local belief is that the MOUNTAINEER lost its wheels and became a stationary engine serving some village industry. Abandonment was complete.

Who would believe, after this abject and humiliating downfall, that many years later a new railroad would succeed where the Canajoharie & Catskill had failed?

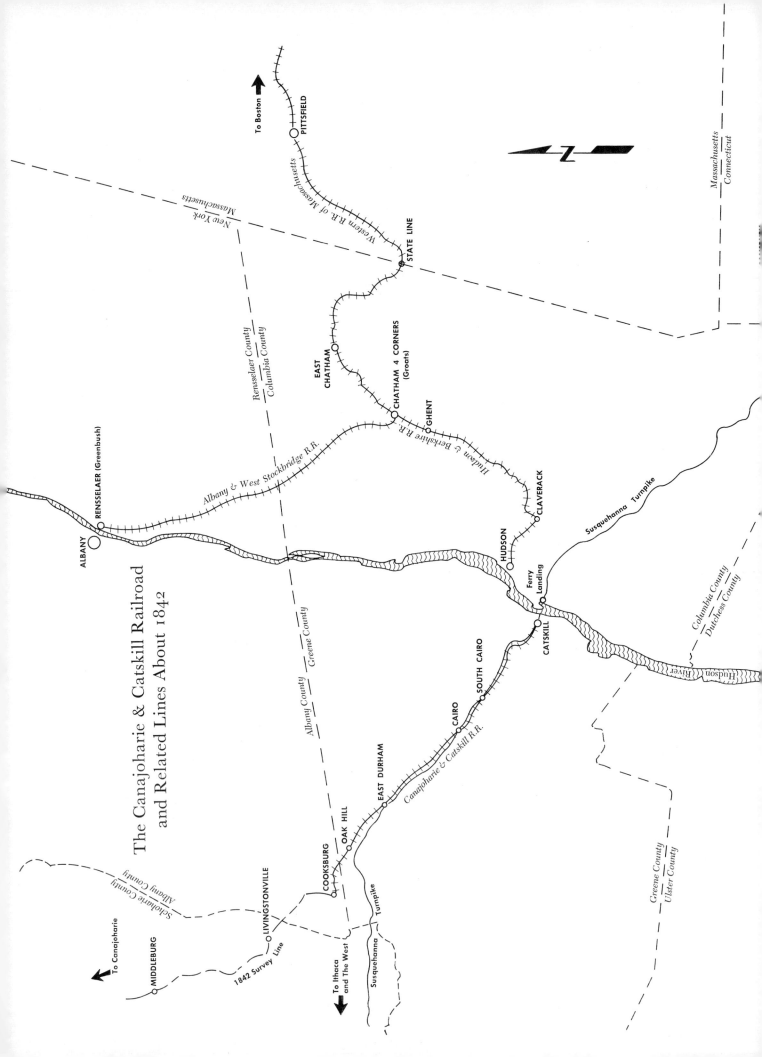

The Canajoharie & Catskill Railroad
and Related Lines About 1842

To Boston
PITTSFIELD

Western R.R. of Massachusetts

STATE LINE

Massachusetts
Connecticut

New York
Massachusetts

Rensselaer County
Columbia County

EAST CHATHAM

CHATHAM 4 CORNERS
(Groats)

GHENT

Hudson & Berkshire R.R.

RENSSELAER (Greenbush)

Albany & West Stockbridge R.R.

CLAVERACK

ALBANY

HUDSON

Ferry Landing

Columbia County
Dutchess County

Susquehanna Turnpike

CATSKILL

Hudson River

Albany County
Greene County

SOUTH CAIRO

CAIRO

Canajoharie & Catskill R.R.

Greene County
Ulster County

EAST DURHAM

OAK HILL

COOKSBURG

LIVINGSTONVILLE

Schoharie County
Albany County

1842 Survey Line

To Ithaca
and The West

Susquehanna Turnpike

To Canajoharie

MIDDLEBURG

CHAPTER FIVE

The Trackless Pathway

HE closing down of operations on the Canajoharie & Catskill was symptomatic of the increasingly uneasy partnership between New York State and private transportation enterprise. When, on May 20, 1842, both the C. & C. and the Ithaca & Owego went under the hammer, the state suffered a staggering loss. The loan of public credit to these lines had been a failure, and public opinion began to change.

Even Governor William Bouck, an advocate of internal improvements in general and the Canajoharie & Catskill in particular, had second thoughts. Standing soberly at the legislative rostrum on January 3, 1843, he warned against "extravagant expenditures or ill-advised undertakings."[1] Whereas the legislators had felt pressure from the "sequestered counties" (those areas with no easy access to the Erie Canal) for better transportation, a counter-pressure now developed as a reaction to substantial drains on the state treasury. New York's pride in "Clinton's Ditch" had led to a proliferation of canal and railroad projects, all of which required either state funding (for the canals) or the loan of public credit (for the railroads). Inevitably, the day of reckoning came.

In 1842, all public works in the state were suspended. Four years later the Constitutional Convention pushed through an article denying direct state aid to any private corporation.

Thus, the Canajoharie line fell victim not only to its own inherent problems but to legislative disenchantment with all such visionary schemes. Its counterpart to the east, the Hudson & Berkshire Rail Road had, before 1842, undergone similar trials in its brief life. Surprisingly, it did not suffer the same fate, but sustained itself in one way or another until the present day.

Like the C. & C., the Hudson road was surveyed by Army Engineers in 1828 and 1829, its purpose being to connect the Hudson River with the Western Railroad of Massachusetts, whose eastern terminal was Boston and the Atlantic Ocean. Incorporated in 1832 and aided by issuance of state railroad stock in the amount of $150,000 (Laws of 1840, Chapter 178), the line opened for travel between Hudson and State Line in September, 1838. Its construction was as unpretentious as that of the Canajoharie road: wooden rails with strap iron capping, grades of up to 80 feet to the mile, curves "crooked as a ram's horn," and fragile timber trestles. Spring floods damaged its embankments and carried away its bridges in 1839 and 1840 and deficit financing characterized its early years.[2]

It had, however, some advantages not shared by the C. & C. From the beginning, it appears to have had substantial local support and no taint of scandal. Also, it formed a connecting link for the Western Railroad of Massachusetts, which needed a convenient western outlet. Hudson village enjoyed a spurt of business activity during 1841 and 1842 while the Western ran its trains over the Hudson & Berkshire. Unfortunately, the arrangement was quickly discontinued. An easier, more level and less tortuous route to the shipping center at Albany was found and utilized by the Albany & West Stockbridge. This alternate route followed gentle grades and moderate curves north from Groat's Tavern (Chatham Four Corners) to Greenbush, across the river from Albany. At that busy transportation center, the west-bound Boston traffic met river steamers, canal boats, three turnpikes and the Mohawk & Hudson Railroad. The Berkshire route survived, barely, as a local branch line of the Western Railroad.[3]

Disappointing though this may have been to Hudson and Columbia County, Catskill and Greene County had cause for even greater cha-

A reminder of the old railroad. This culvert near Leeds may be seen from Route 23. The loose stone is from C. & C. construction; the more modern slabs below are from the Catskill Mountain Railroad improvement. *(Photograph by the author)*

"High on the face of South Mountain, . . . the eye, by looking very keenly, sees a small speck, hanging like a swallow's nest to a wall. If we look through a pair of good glasses, you will see that it is a spacious hotel, and that on its piazzas are gathered perhaps several hundred human beings, looking out over the magnificent landscape, which spreads like a map below them, and watching the thread of silver that gleams occasionally in the far distance, marking the course of the Hudson." *(Our Native Land,* 1882)

grin. The once-prosperous business area was rapidly becoming a stagnant economic backwater. Its productive crop lands were being overworked. Its rich pastures were thinning from sheep grazing. Its hemlock forests were vanishing in the tanners' wake. Its docks were deteriorating from lack of use. Even though dairy farms, bluestone quarries, brickyards and flour mills took up some of the slack, trade back from the river banks stagnated into local, small-scale transactions. To a large extent, the territory's period of business expansion was at an end.

In the decade between 1860 and 1870, the population of New York State swelled by half a million; Greene County lost one hundred residents.[4] Both Thomas B. Cooke and Ephraim Beach had already departed this life, in 1853 and 1857, their deaths removing two Catskill reminders of the ruined railroad.[5]

To offset this adversity, citizens could point to a white speck near the mountain horizon, a sparkling jewel suspended between the peaks, the Catskill Mountain House. This impressive hostelry with its gleaming facade of thirteen Corinthian columns was enjoying great popularity and a virtual monopoly in the Catskills. In the absence of other means of access, the steamboat landing at Catskill accommodated almost all travelers en route to the inn under the clouds. The greater number of these passenger ships flew the flag of the company whose name soon became synonymous with swift and elegant river travel — the Hudson River Day Line. Under the firm business hand of Alfred Van Santvoord, of an old Hudson-Dutch family, the company prospered and Van Santvoord himself became a heavy investor in Catskill's new transportation system.[6]

Despite the C. & C. fiasco of 1842, Catskillians saw a need for better transportation into the Catskill Mountains. The old Susquehanna Turnpike company relinquished its control and its maintenance of the route in the 1850's, and the dirt roads diverging from it south and then west up the mountainsides were poorly kept. Stagecoaches of uncertain vintage rolled along the old mountain road for about a half a day before depositing sore, dusty and exhausted passengers at the lofty Mountain House. The most arduous part of the visitor's trip consisted of the tedious, bone-shaking journey

of twelve miles from landing to mountain top. From a humanitarian standpoint, if from no other, there was a need to ease the traveler's discomfort. And there were other, more hard-headed arguments for a smoother, speedier ride to the resort area.

By 1870, the Catskill Mountain House was no longer alone. The monopoly was broken by a spate of hotel construction in the Catskills. Many of the rival structures appeared on promontories in southern Greene County and west of the original Pine Orchard edifice. Enterprising farmers in the entire fan-shaped area above New York City, particularly in Sullivan, Delaware, Orange and Ulster counties, had long recognized that supplementary income could be produced by renting out spare rooms to summer boarders. The Erie Railroad furnished these boarders with a convenient access route to these boardinghouses in the Shawungunk Mountains and in the foothills of the Catskills. But the Erie simply skirted the potential resort area; other railroads would exploit it.

The demands upon men, material and money during the Civil War had halted new railroad construction in the state. But a renewal of the epidemic railroad fever occurred once these wartime demands had been satisfied. Two projects in particular promised to open up the lower Catskills, to provide a convenient door to the southern mountains. In the late sixties, surveys located a new railroad between Middletown in Orange County and Oswego on Lake Ontario. And from the Hudson River port of Kingston a line was run to the Albany & Susquehanna Railroad at Oneonta. Both routes would draw upon the previously-untapped resources, natural and agricultural, of the territory south of the Mountain House and downstream from Catskill. Both routes would snake north and west, effectively detouring some freight and passenger traffic away from the Hudson River, at least beyond Kingston. And though railroads did not create prosperity, they made it easier to come by. Particularly pleased were the boardinghouse operators and hotel owners who had railroad transportation at their very doorstep. The resort business boomed.

The Oswego line, the more ambitious (and less fortunate) of the two, took the name New York & Oswego Midland Railroad. It became, in time, an important passenger carrier for the Jewish resort area, the Borscht Belt. Although the Oswego Midland survived for the greater part of a century as the New York, Ontario & Western Railway, it resembled a somewhat more successful Canajoharie & Catskill. As a shortcut between New York City and the west, it had a contorted right-of-way, it experienced severe financial difficulties, it gained a scandalous reputation, it failed and abandoned its line. But during its prosperous years, it was a major artery for summer travel.

The other embankment, that of the Rondout & Oswego, bisected Ulster and Delaware Counties (and later boasted of this in a new corporate title, the Ulster & Delaware Railroad). This line entered directly into the Catskills but did not touch the heart of the summer vacation land, still centered at and near the "venerable" Catskill Mountain House. Nevertheless, it formed an alternate route to the peaks in Greene County and it encouraged investment in substantial summer hotels along the Ulster & Delaware. By 1880, the southern perimeter of the mountains was dotted with vacation lodges, large and small. From West Hurley station, for example, stages ran to the Overlook Mountain House, 3,800 feet above the river, three stories high and 200 feet long. The view was said to be over 100 miles. At the other extreme in size and appointments was the Woodland Cottage, which accepted "a few select boarders" at Phoenicia.[7] There was truly gold in them thar hills.

Competition of this kind worried Greene County as a tourist area and Catskill as a port of entry. The railroad improvements in Ulster, Delaware, Orange and Sullivan Counties attracted vacationers who might otherwise accept the longer steamboat junket and the grueling stagecoach journey to the mountain tops by way of Catskill. The southern threat was immediate and growing. Something had to be done, but with the Canajoharie & Catskill still not forgotten, caution was the watchword.

Caution was underlined by the financial panic of 1873, but the desire to eliminate the poor trans-portation facilities between Catskill Landing and the Greene County mountain resorts remained. By 1879 even the most conservative men were convinced that a railroad must be built. Casting about for economy in construction and operation, the promoters saw immediately that much of the old Canajoharie roadbed could be used. They also noted that freight would be but a fraction of the expected income and that summer visitors would be the richest cargo. However, the cost of building another standard gauge line was prohibitive and the winding route a challenge. They decided upon narrow gauge.

Narrow gauge, or the light railway, had gained adherents in England and North America for many reasons. Construction costs would be reduced by nearly half, natural land contours could be followed more closely by a restricted width of track, equipment could be smaller and more economical in operation and related savings could be realized. The Denver & Rio Grande Railway was the pioneer narrow gauge route in the United States, but even New York State had its representatives. By 1876 there were four: Central Valley (Bainbridge to Smithville Flats), Bath & Hammondsport, Crown Point (to serve the Iron Company ore beds) and Peekskill Valley (from the Hudson River Railroad to the iron furnaces). For its limited objective, to shuttle passengers from the steamboats to the foot of the mountains, the narrow gauge seemed an admirable choice.[8]

As might be expected, the proprietors of the Catskill Mountain House expressed early interest in the venture. Charles L. Beach, who with his father Erastus had controlled the Albany-New York stage and mail lines, was now the principal owner of the Mountain House and a strong supporter of the new railroad venture.[9] The Van Santvoords of New York City, owners of the Hudson River Day Line, came forward in support of the project. Enthusiasm was general and the outlook was bright.

The trackless pathway of another day would have shining new iron and feel the weight of passing trains once more.

41

Three Catskill boats. The ferryboat *A. F. Beach,* freighter *W. C. Redfield* and passenger liner *Kaaterskill* make a tranquil picture at the Landing. *(Donald Ringwald Collection)*

CHAPTER SIX

Rip's Depot

BETWEEN 1842 and 1880, the commercial development of the Catskills was slight except for the burgeoning hotel business. Movement of the tanneries and flour mills westward, closer to the remaining hemlock forests and the vast midwest grain fields, had left an economic gap that would never be completely filled. Efforts to stimulate trade and improve trade channels came to naught.

In the late 1860's and into the 1870's several schemes were aired to rejuvenate the old Canajoharie & Catskill. To some the old roadbed was a kind of shameful wound, still painful, across the face of Greene County. To others, the ready-made cuts and embankments were symbolic of an opportunity lost, a road not taken. No fewer than three attempts were made to reopen the line. The Catskill & Middleburgh, the Catskill & Schoharie Valley and the Catskill & Schoharie all intended to carry out Governor Bouck's aim of entering the fertile valley of the Schoharie. Here the line would also connect with the Schoharie Valley Railroad (1865) and Middleburgh & Schoharie Railroad (1867) which met the Delaware & Hudson, a main line to the north and south, at Central Bridge. None of these enterprises was ever translated from paper work to iron rails.

Probably wiser heads saw that the area's principal asset was not its freight possibilities but its passenger certainties. Several miles back from the Hudson shore, the resort houses were strung out on a line beginning at the lofty Mountain House and rolling back for about ten miles, past picturesque Kaaterskill Falls and the precipitous cascade at Haines' Corners. These same mountain ledges, from which the water courses discharged their clear torrents, drew thousands of awe-struck tourists. Even today the dizzying prospects from the Overlook, Newman's Ledge, Sunset Rock, North Point, Inspiration Point and Mountain House ledge cannot fail to impress. Clearly, these visitors must have easy access to this elevated vacation land.

On the afternoon of September 9, 1880, a spirited meeting was held in Werner's law offices to formulate plans for a railroad from Catskill to the mountains. John Bagley, Jr. was named chairman and George H. Stevens secretary of the meeting. That this was more than a discussion group was apparent; those attending subscribed $75,000 worth of stocks and bonds.[1] By the end of the month, the newly organized Catskill Mountain Railroad Company had engaged Charles E. Fogg, a civil engineer from Poughkeepsie, to run the survey between Catskill Landing and Palenville. He was retracing Ephraim Beach's steps before the week was out.[2]

Among the promoters of the Catskill Mountain Railroad was Charles L. Beach, the sagacious entrepreneur who owned and operated the Catskill Mountain House. His early investment of $100,000 assured him of the post of President even if his acknowledged executive ability did not.[3] He presided at a meeting held in the village in November when the construction was laid out in sections: section 1 from the Point to Van Hoesen's Falls, section 2 from there to R. M. Lawrence's, section 3 to Palenville. Theodore Beach, Seymour Adams and Theodore Teale were appointed to obtain rights-of-way for their respective sections.[4]

Anticipating the advent of another railroad project from Catskill, the local press not only gave the project prominent space and ample coverage, but an occasional gratuitous remark:

> All the conductors on the Indianapolis and Jeffersonville RR. have been discharged for stealing. This should be a timely warning to the conductors on the Catskill Mountain RR.[5]

Why the *Examiner* editor should feel compelled to

CATSKILL MOUNTAIN RAILROAD

FROM CATSKILL LANDING, on the Hudson River, TO THE CATSKILL MOUNTAINS.

SHORTEST, QUICKEST and MOST DESIRABLE ROUTE

To or from the Catskill Mountain House, Hotel Kaaterskill, Laurel House, Haines's Falls, TANNERSVILLE, Palenville, Cairo, Durham, Windham and Other Points in the Catskill Mountain Region.

Passengers for HOTEL KAATERSKILL and CATSKILL MOUNTAIN HOUSE will reach either Hotel TWO HOURS EARLIER BY THIS ROUTE than practicable by any other.

☞ Guests can Breakfast after 8 a.m. at the above Hotels and reach New York by this Route at 2:15 p.m.

TIME, EXPENSE AND OVER 50 MILES OF TRAVEL SAVED BY THIS ROUTE TO TOURISTS FROM OR TO SARATOGA.

Summer Boarders returning from TANNERSVILLE and vicinity should not fail to drive down the Mountains THROUGH THE FAMOUS KAATERSKILL CLOVE and take passage by this Road from Palenville to Catskill.

Close Connections at Catskill with HUDSON RIVER DAY LINE STEAMERS, STEAMERS OF THE CATSKILL NIGHT LINE, N. Y. C. & HUDSON RIVER RAILROAD AND N. Y., WEST SHORE & B. RAILWAY.

	LEAVE			ARRIVE		
	P.M.	A.M.	A.M.	P.M.	P.M.	P.M.
NEW YORK	6.00	9 and 11	9.00	2.15 & 5.30	7.00 & 7.40	9.20
SARATOGA		1 P.M.	8.40	2.25	6.15 & 8.20	9.00
ALBANY	5.15 A.M.	2 P.M.	10.20	1.00	4.05 & 6.10	7.45

TIME-TABLE NO. 7.
Takes Effect Monday, Sept. 10th, 1883.

CATSKILL TO PALENVILLE.

DISTANCES	STATIONS.	No. 1. CATSKILL NIGHT LINE EXPRESS. A.M.	No. 3. N Y C & H R RR EXPRESS. P.M.	No. 5. DAY LINE AND RAILROAD EXPRESS. A.M.
	Leave ..CATSKILL LAND'G.. Arrive	7.25	12.25	3.40
1	....CATSKILL VILLAGE....	7.30	12.30	3.45
2	WEST SHORE STATION	7.33		3.48
6	....LEEDS....			
8	...SOUTH CAIRO...	7.55	12.55	4.10
12	...LAWRENCEVILLE...			
14	MOUNTAIN HOUSE ST'N	8.15	1.15	4.30
16	Arrive ..PALENVILLE.. Leave	8.25	1.25	4.40
		A.M.	P.M.	P.M.

PALENVILLE TO CATSKILL.

DISTANCES	STATIONS.	No. 2. DAY LINE AND RAILROAD EXPRESS. A.M.	No. 4. AFTERNOON EXPRESS. P.M.	No. 6. NIGHT LINE AND RAILROAD EXPRESS. P.M.
16	Leave ..CATSKILL LAND'G.. Arrive	10.40	2.40	5.55
15	....CATSKILL VILLAGE....	10.35	2.35	5.50
15	WEST SHORE STATION	10.32	2.32	
10	....LEEDS....			
8	...SOUTH CAIRO...	10.10	2.10	5.25
4	...LAWRENCEVILLE...			
2	MOUNTAIN HOUSE ST'N	9.50	1.50	5.05
	Arrive ..PALENVILLE.. Leave	9.40	1.40	4.55
		A.M.	P.M.	P.M.

* Trains No. 1 and No. 6 will run on SUNDAYS and MONDAYS. Train No. 1 will run on ONE HOUR LATER TIME on SUNDAYS and MONDAYS.

On SATURDAYS only a Special Train will leave Catskill Landing at 7 P.M., to connect with trains of the N. Y. C. & H. R. R. RR., which leave New York at 3.30 P.M., Saratoga at 4 P.M. and Albany at 5.25 P.M. Connection with this train can also be made from Saratoga at 4 P.M. and Albany at 5.30 P.M. via N. Y., WEST SHORE & B. Ry. This train will run on regular time and stop at all regular stations.

A —— indicates that trains stop only on signal or to let off passengers.

THROUGH TICKETS FOR SALE AND BAGGAGE CHECKED FOR NEW YORK VIA ALL LINES!

From Palenville, Mountain House Station and South Cairo; also from Walters Brothers' Hotel, Cairo, via Cairo Stage Line, connecting with Railroad at South Cairo.

Tickets for Saratoga, Philadelphia, Baltimore and Washington for Sale at Palenville and Mountain House Station.

For small time-tables containing further information address

CHAS. A. BEACH, SUPERINTENDENT,
CATSKILL, N. Y.

Timetable (Courtesy Greene Co. Historical Society)

issue such a warning, before a tie had been placed or a rail laid, is puzzling. It may have been just railroad-consciousness or it may have been a distorted echo from the past, a subconscious memory of the C. & C. humiliation.

An undated pamphlet of these early years raised the estimate of total cost for the venture from $75,000 (the newspaper speculation after the September 9 meeting) to almost $300,000. Grading and superstructure was to cost $100,000, iron for bridges $27,000, 40 pound rails $71,750, stations and structures $5,000, land costs $20,000 and engineering (plus legal expenses) $16,000. Equipment projections were $17,000 for two 25-ton locomotives and $33,000 for 30 cars (10 passenger, 4 baggage, 12 freight and 4 flat).

This substantial increase in the projected expenditures must have given Catskill citizens some second thoughts. And the delay in completion of the road improved the pessimistic prospect not a whit.

Late in December of 1880, the Catskill Company signed a contract with O'Brien and Rogers for construction of 15¾ miles of railroad, exclusive of bridges, between the Point at Catskill and Palenville. Ground was to be broken about January 15 and the last spike to be driven by June 1 of 1881. Work was to start at Luke Van Vechten's (south of Leeds), and then three gangs were to be put to work at the Point, at Wolcott's Mills and at Neely Lawrence's.[6] At about this time residents of the town of Durham saw the chance to revive the Canajoharie & Catskill. On January 8, the *Examiner* reported the committee deliberations at the Irving House which resulted in the formation of the South Cairo & East Durham Company, the westerly termination of which would eliminate the need for the four bridges (including the infamous High Rock span).[7] All in all, the village and the county welcomed the new transportation enterprise.

The railroad was not an isolated phenomenon, an independent company depending upon local accommodation. It was actually a link in a water-rail-hotel amalgamation, in which the Mountain House's Charles L. Beach was deeply involved. Beach's former ties with the Albany to New York stagecoach lines, a most successful venture, boded well for the three-foot railroad company he

headed. And representing the river transportation interests were two men from New York City, Alfred Van Santvoord and Charles L. Rickerson. Van Santvoord's main concern was the Hudson River Day Line, the *prima donna* of the steamboat traffic on the river; Rickerson's was the Catskill Evening Line (more properly, the Catskill & New York Steamboat Company, Limited) a local freight and passenger service for Catskill, Hudson and Coxsackie. Among the sidewheelers whose home port was Catskill were the *City of Catskill* and *City of Hudson* with passengers and the *W. C. Redfield* and *Thomas McManus* with freight — all flying the Catskill Evening Line flag.[8] When the railroad was completed, the work of carting people and goods from the docks would be no longer exclusively the monopoly of horsedrawn vehicles, lumbering freight wagons and shabby omnibuses. The railroad would lay its rails right down to the waterfront.

In February the construction gang had reached Dunham's boathouse and had driven the first pile in the swamp above the Long Dock. An agreement with the Power Bridge Company of Troy for $28,000 was reached for the erection of the three bridges over the creek. All along the route dust was rising. Not without minor casualty, however, as Milton Palmer's family discovered. The Palmer house stood close to the roadbed in Jefferson and closer still to an enormous buttonball tree. The contractor insisted on the removal of the tree, attached a guy rope to control its fall (preferably away from the house and nearby fruit trees) and applied axe and saw to the task. The rope parted and the falling tree carried away the Palmer roof, demolishing the second story in the process. The accident proved more embarrassing than injurious, fortunately.[9]

In order to reach the landing place of the palatial Day Liners, the Catskill Mountain Railroad track extended beyond the old terminus of the Canajoharie & Catskill. In the early 1800's, the narrow neck of water between a small island in the Hudson and Catskill village had been filled by landowners along the waterfront — Peter Mesick, John Thomson, James Powers and others. Now that the gap was bridged, the fast steamers no longer entered the mouth of Catskill Creek, preferring to tie up alongside the more convenient dock at the Landing, the eastern side of what had once been an island. Between this little peninsula and the village was a high rock ridge. To get from the former C. & C. end of track and the Point required a deep cut that became the most ambitious excavation on the line. Blasting the porous rock proved so tricky that the entire summer was spent in pick and shovel work. Reports on the progress of this drudgery appeared in the *Examiner* from February to August. The difficulty may be judged (in part) by the strike of the workers in February for a raise from $1.00 a day to $1.50. That the company granted this increase is further evidence of the stubbornness of this obstacle.[10]

Actually, the railroad management had chosen the kind of railroad that would require the very least in cost and construction. Their selection of the narrow gauge, despite Palmer's buttonball tree and the cut at the Landing, seemed to be the proper one.

Even so, June came and went, July passed and August declined without a sign of a train. Rails — 30 feet long, 40 pounds to the yard — began to arrive in the late fall of 1881, long after the target date of completion, June 1.[11] Equipment remained to be purchased and the arrangement with the South Cairo & East Durham company had yet to be made. The S. C. & E. D. committee, becoming restive, announced in the *Examiner* for December 24:

> It is of vital importance to the welfare of both companies, and to the county, that perfect harmony and a mutual good understanding between all parties should exist. It was the lack of this element in the old Canajoharie road that brought it to grief and put Catskill back in the dark ages.

The backers of the South Cairo & East Durham were to be disappointed, for the extension was never built. There were other projects of more immediate concern to the railroad supporters.

Two new steamships for the Catskill Evening Line slid off the ways, ready to accept passengers on the Catskill to New York route. *The City of Catskill* had made its appearance on the river in 1880 and the *Kaaterskill* (pronounced "Kawterskill" by the knowledgeable) steamed up the Hudson in 1882. The *Catskill* was 250 feet long, 35 feet 8 inches wide, with a wooden hull and a Fletcher steam engine. Her massive dimensions and elegant appointments made her the most impressive boat on the Evening Line. On the night of November 8, 1881, the *Catskill* found herself fogged in just north of New York City, along with the *St. John* and *Saratoga*, two rival steamers. When the fog lifted, the three captains determined to make up lost time and to see who could outrun

The *Kaaterskill* at Albany. This side view of her 265-foot length shows the large hog frames and extensive paddle housing. *(Steamship Historical Society of America, Inc.)*

The Main Street cut. This fern-fringed slot connected Catskill village and the Landing by rail. No. 2 just barely clears the rock walls. (*Author's collection*)

the other two. The race was on. Dense smoke rolled and curled from each stack and the paddlewheels churned up white water. The *St. John,* with a reputation for great speed, led the three until Newburgh came into sight. As the belching river monsters passed the coal dock, the *Catskill* pulled ahead of the *Saratoga* in a shower of smoke and cinders. She retained her lead for the rest of the run up the river, overhauling the *St. John* near Poughkeepsie.[12] Her reputation was established and the Evening Line gained stature.

The *City of Catskill's* days of fame were numbered, however, for she burned at Rondout dock less than two years later. Her sister ship, the *Kaaterskill,* only slightly larger, made her last trip in 1913, after many years of passenger service.[13] The management renamed their 1863-vintage *Escort* as the *City of Catskill,* but the name seemed to bring bad luck, for she was rammed by the *St.*

John in New York Harbor in 1897, sunk and was raised for repair. Sensibly, the company abandoned the name, and the *Escort-Catskill* became the *City of Hudson.*[14]

The land link for these river steamers was still incomplete in early 1882, but progress was being made. The bridge contractors continued erection work into January, despite a high gale that blew down telephone and telegraph wires and dislodged the center span of the railroad bridge at the village. The span was replaced and the bridge gang labored on through the blustery winter. There was good reason for this apparent disregard of the elements.[15]

Other construction was underway not far distant from Catskill. The Stony Clove & Catskill Mountain Railroad was creeping north from its connection with the Ulster & Delaware at Phoenicia. This fourteen-mile narrow gauge line would

47

terminate at Hunter, nearly on a level with the Catskill Mountain House and within ten miles of it.[16] There was reason for haste and cause for irritation. Costs were rising and problems were developing.

Driving a cut through the stubborn stone near the Landing was bothersome enough, but the swampy ground between it and the dock also presented a difficulty. It could not possibly support the weight of trains, even the nimble little narrow gauge processions. So the company was forced to hire the Power Bridge Company to drive 650 piles into the bog. At the same time they made final plans to build a two-story depot on the Hinman farm at Palenville.[17] Rolling stock was expected to arrive any day.

To run its trains, the Catskill Mountain Railroad hired its first operating employee. One bit of good luck came to the management when they took on John L. Driscoll as master mechanic and engineer in April of 1882. A veteran of almost twenty years of engine service, Driscoll had started as a fireman on the Hudson River Railroad and most recently had filled the post of master mechanic on the Poughkeepsie & Eastern.[18] He was on hand to supervise the unloading of the first shipment of equipment. On April 26 the canal boat *Cyrus Lord* delivered twelve cars — 2 box, 4 flat with rack sides, 4 work-flat cars and 2 unidentified cars — from the Jackson & Sharp Company of Wilmington, Delaware. Driscoll supervised the laying of temporary track to Lee's stone dock where the transfer was made. Within the month the first locomotive was landed here, and No. 1, the S. SHERWOOD DAY, rumbled onto dry land and went to work.[19] Its rambles between the Point and the first bridge attracted crowds of young daredevils. An incensed *Examiner* editor reported on June 3rd that about "1,000 hoodlums" were dodging in and about the engine and work cars, disregarding frequent steam baths from the engine. More calmly, he noted that the first conductor had been hired, W. Irving Osborn, "the right man in the right place."

The deadline for the opening for traffic had now passed and the only passengers carried had been the company officials and the foolhardy "hoodlums" — between Greene Street and the stone dock. The temporary tracks and sidings were rapidly filling with equipment, ties and rails. During the month of June the newspaper accounted for 10 passenger cars to add to the freight equipment and the two locomotives (the JOHN T. MANN, No. 2, had arrived shortly after the DAY). The passenger cars were fully described. The exteriors were a gleaming dark green and the lettering was in gold paint outlined in vermillion. They seated 48 persons in 12 double seats and four long benches lengthwise of the car at the ends. The interiors had ash woodwork and the seats were upholstered in crimson and green plush with nickle-plated arms and tops. All were equipped with Janney couplers, compression buffers (a continental touch) and Eames vacuum brakes. But their wheels were not to roll until nearly the end of the summer.

On Saturday afternoon, July 29, 1882, the railroad was opened to the public and the first passenger train rolled from the Day Line dock over the low swamp trestle, through the narrow rock cut, crossed Greene Street with triumphant little toots and stopped at Bridge Street, at its downtown waiting room. In taking up the slack, Engineer Driscoll broke a coupling and the train was delayed until repairs were made. Nevertheless, the trip to Lawrenceville (Neely Lawrence's) was accomplished in about one hour. There and at South Cairo, stages waited for patronage, travelers bound for the mountain resorts or for Cairo and the upper reaches of Catskill Creek. The second trip of the day was to leave the Landing at 8 p.m., just after the arrival of the night boat, the much-touted *Kaaterskill*.[20]

Even the new river liner had its share of bad luck on this first trip from New York. Leaving the pier at 1 p.m., the *Kaaterskill* plowed along at good speed until she reached West Point. There the new Fletcher engine became overheated and steam was shut off until her parts cooled down, a matter of about two hours. The crowd which had gathered to watch the *Kaaterskill* arrive at Catskill Landing impatiently waited for the sound of the whistle downriver. On the tracks nearby a crew kept the engine hot for the train of five cars, one baggage car and four coaches. Finally the *Kaaterskill* smoked into sight at about ten minutes past ten o'clock. A cannon drawn up close to the shore boomed out Catskill's greeting,

In Austin's Glen. A varnish run negotiates one of the frequent bends along Catskill Creek, following the line originally run by the Canajoharie & Catskill. The abandoned paper mill stood at center left. *(Author's collection)*

fireworks lit up the water and the massed spectators cheered. Within minutes about 200 people piled onto the brand-new little train, for its second trip down the line. This time the run was made without incident.[21]

The first few days of railroad operation had their minor, annoying incidents — a derailment near Leeds, hotel runners detouring passengers from the boats onto stages and a few local "croakers" who were lectured in the local press:

> The building of the Canajoharie & Catskill was a greater enterprise and had a larger scope than the undertaking of the Catskill Mountain R. R. Let us be just to those who in that early day sought to develop our resources. Had they succeeded this village today would have been one of the most flourishing on the Hudson. They did not. Politics crept in and speedy disorganization followed.[22]

With the backing of the Mountain House, Day Line and Evening Line interests, there was little chance that the railroad would fail as its predecessor had. The only real threat to its existence came from another railroad.

On the same Saturday that the *Kaaterskill* docked at Catskill and the Catskill Mountain Railroad sent out its first train, a similar celebration was held in Hunter, the terminus of the Stony Clove & Catskill Mountain Railroad.[23] The C. M. line was still unfinished; about three miles was the distance from Lawrenceville to the Mountain House. The Stony Clove route put passengers within ten miles of it. Before many weeks had passed, the Catskill company had laid its rails to Mountain House Station, the point where the old stage route to the Mountain House was intersected.

49

RULES AND REGULATIONS, CATSKILL MOUNTAIN RAILROAD.

1. The Standard Time is kept by the clock at the depot on Catskill Point. Conductors and Engineers must keep their time in exact conformity to it.

2. Trains must not leave Stations before the time specified on time-table, nor must they arrive in advance of the table time at any Station at which arriving time is given.

Construction Trains must keep out of the way of Passenger Trains.

3. All Trains bound East will have the right of track for thirty (30) minutes beyond their time, as per time-table, after which Trains going West will have the right to proceed, but must not make up any of the time lost in waiting until delayed train is passed. To prevent the chance of accidents arising from the variation of watches, all Subordinate Trains must reach the place of meeting at least three (3) minutes before the table time of starting for the Train having the right of track, which Train must wait five (5) minutes past its table time for the Subordinate Train. The five (5) minutes allowed for safety at the place of meeting must be observed until Subordinate Train is passed.

4. Freight Trains must keep out of the way of Passenger Trains at least ten (10) minutes and must wait indefinitely for them.

5. Any Extra or Irregular Train or Engine, whether under flag or otherwise, must keep out of the way of all Regular Trains and will never have the right of track over any Regular Train on any part of the road.

6. No Train or Detached Engine following another shall leave a station within ten (10) minutes of a preceding Train, but must keep at least ten (10) minutes behind and proceed with caution. This rule is imperative; and Engineers must come to a full stop within ten (10) minutes.

SIGNALS.

7. A RED FLAG by day and a RED LANTERN or other light swung by night are signals of danger and indicate that the train must stop.

8. RED AND WHITE signals shown together are signals of caution and indicate that the train must run slowly.

9. A RED FLAG carried on the forward end of Engine by day and a RED LIGHT similarly carried by night denotes an Extra Train or Engine following, which must keep out of the way of all Regular Trains. Two of these signals must always be carried, to guard against the chances of one falling off or becoming extinguished.

10. The signal to GO AHEAD is the waving of the Arm or White Light over the head. The signal to STOP is the moving of the Arm or any Light straight up and down. The signal to BACK is the moving of the Arm or Light to and fro across the track.

11. ONE short quick blast of the whistle signifies APPLY the brakes. Two short quick blasts signify LOOSEN the brakes. THREE short quick blasts signify BACK the Train.

12. All Trains will approach Stations and run over Bridges and through the village of Catskill with reduced speed and with care.

13. At regular meeting-places the first train arriving at a Station will take the side track, entering from the nearest end.

14. Remember, in all cases of doubt or uncertainty, to take the safe course and run no risk.

15. Conductors will see that their Cars are kept neat and clean; that the Brakemen do not slide the wheels; that the Bell-Cord is unobstructed throughout and properly attached to the Engine; that all Switches used by them are locked upon the Main Track before leaving; THAT A BRAKEMAN IS ALWAYS STATIONED ON THE REAR CAR with a Red Flag by day and a Red Lantern by night; and that they have on their Trains sufficient train tools and supplies.

16. Engineers must not permit any person to ride on the Engine except the proper officers of the Road when on duty, *without orders*.

17. Engineers approaching a Station will blow one long blast of whistle and pass the Switches cautiously; and at Road-Crossings will blow two blasts of whistle and ring the Bell continually within eighty (80) rods.

18. Engineers must understand all orders for movement of their Engines before starting and must personally answer to all train orders addressed to them.

19. Track-repairers are required to give notice of any obstruction by their work a sufficient distance from the same each way; and Engineers are enjoined to proceed with extreme caution when such notice is given until the obstruction is passed.

20. The use of Intoxicating Drink on the Road or about the premises of the corporation is strictly prohibited.

21. Brakemen must remember always to disconnect Bell-Cords and the Hose attached to the Vacuum Brakes whenever Cars are uncoupled.

22. The Head-Lights of Engines running after dark must be lighted.

CHAS. A. BEACH, Superintendent.

While Lawrenceville was still the end of track, a writer for *Harper's New Monthly Magazine* entrained at the Landing and alighted at the foot of the mountains:

> A curious scene presents itself at the railway terminus. Although nothing is finished yet, the traveler demands swift locomotion, and so things have been put in working order in advance of their actual completion. With High Peak rising grandly at his back, with the rush of a mountain torrent in his ears, with a stretch of richly rolling country to right and left, silent with the silence of majestic supremacy, the ticket agent sits out-of-doors, with a little pine table before him whence he distributes tickets.[24]

Even before the entire 15.73 miles of slim gauge track was in regular use, a branch road was under consideration. Not as ambitious as the South Cairo & East Durham, the Cairo Railroad would at least strike out in the same direction. During the early winter, two surveys were run. The first was over the C. & C.'s original embankment by way of Dennis Stewart's farm and through the valley, the second from a point south of the creek on a long straight line.[25]

Railroad operations ceased for the season on October 21st and the results were examined. The annual earnings report released by the company in December was hardly encouraging:

Capital stock	$100,000.00
Capital stock paid in	77,800.00
Number of stockholders	33
Debts	41,990.86
Cost of road and equipment	313,873.51
Bonds authorized	200,000.00
Bonds issued	198,000.00
Earnings in 1882	8,105.19
Charges against earnings	5,388.45
Surplus	2,716.74

Nevertheless, the primary purpose of the railroad was to serve as an incentive to vacationers to take the steamboats, to land at Catskill and to lodge at area resort hotels. Profit from the transportation charges would be welcome but was not essential to continuation.

The modest station at Palenville took shape too late for it to be used by passengers in 1882, but in the spring trains would roll into the outskirts of the village.

Rip Van Winkle's town would have a depot.

The miller's house beside the track. A closer view of the scene of the last picture shows the residence of the paper mill proprietor. The old mill foundation at left cannot be seen. (*Winfield W. Robinson Collection at Colgate University*)

THE CATSKILL MOUNTAIN RAILWAY,

From CATSKILL LANDING, on the HUDSON RIVER,

—— TO THE ——

CATSKILL MOUNTAINS,

Is the Shortest, Quickest and Best Route

FROM THE HUDSON RIVER TO THE

Catskill Mountain House and Hotel Kaaterskill, Haines' Falls,
Tannersville, Laurel House, Palenville,
Cairo, Durham, Windham, and Other Points in the
Catskill Mountain Region.

Passengers for **Hotel Kaaterskill** and **Catskill Mountain House** can reach either Hotel
EARLIER BY THIS ROUTE than by any other.

Guests can **Breakfast after** 8 A.M. at the above Hotels and reach New York *by this route* at 2.15 P.M.

Time, Expense and Over Fifty Miles of Travel Saved

By this route to Tourists from or to Saratoga.

Summer Boarders returning from Tannersville and vicinity should not fail to drive down the
Mountains through the **FAMOUS KAATERSKILL CLOVE** and take passage
by this road from Palenville to Catskill.

CLOSE CONNECTION MADE AT CATSKILL

**With the Hudson River Day Line Steamers, and
The Steamers of the Catskill Night Line:
The N. Y. Central & Hudson River R. R. and
West Shore Railroad.**

THREE TRAINS Each Way Daily in June.   **SIX DAILY TRAINS** Each Way in July, August, September.

THROUGH TICKETS should be purchased as follows:

To LEEDS, for Leeds and vicinity.
To CAIRO, *via* the New **CAIRO RAILROAD** Extension, for CAIRO, FREE-
HOLD, EAST DURHAM, OAK HILL, DURHAM, ACRA, SOUTH
DURHAM, EAST WINDHAM AND WINDHAM.
To LAWRENCEVILLE, for Lawrenceville and Kiskatom.
To MOUNTAIN HOUSE STATION, for Catskill Mountain House and Laurel
House.
To PALENVILLE, for Palenville, Hotel Kaaterskill, Haines' Falls, Hilton
House and Tannersville.

Carriages from the above Stations to the various Resorts.

The Railroad and Equipment are first-class in every respect.

THE ROAD WILL BE IN OPERATION during the **SEASON of SUMMER TRAVEL.**

CHAS. A. BEACH, Gen'l Sup't and Pass. Ag't,

CATSKILL, N. Y.

Advertisement from *Van Loan's Catskill Mountain Guide.*

CHAPTER SEVEN

A Slide for Titans

THE YEAR 1883 was, by the only standard available (namely, earnings of 1882) a successful one for the Catskill Mountain Railroad. Even after the season had crested and the hot weather visitors had returned to their homes, the trains were popular. A report turned in by Conductor James B. Tolley on September 15th showed 76 passengers paid $41.50 in fares. Since all trains handled freight, baggage and express, the total receipts for this one movement must have been considerably higher. After the last train of the season had been run, Superintendent Charles A. Beach reported to the Board of Directors that receipts had been $23,500 against operating expenses of about $10,-000. This surplus enabled the company to reduce its debt, to pay interest costs and to defray the construction account.[1]

The extension to Cairo was chartered as a separate corporation on April 10, 1884 with a capitalization of $25,000. As surveyed, from a point about a mile below South Cairo, the route would head northwest into Cairo, about 3.79 miles distant. The project was aimed primarily at increasing freight traffic, which the Catskill Mountain Railroad lacked in any great amount. The road had carried almost 39,000 passengers between May and October, for an income of $19,500. Freight, even with many special lumber trains, produced only about $2,600.[2] Most of the shipments were small and handled easily in the baggage or boxcars coupled into the regular passenger trains. When Cairo was reached, the company expected to load large quantities of bluestone, hay and fruit. And, if traffic warranted, it was hoped that the Cairo-to-Catskill segment could be operated twelve months of the year.

Early in 1885 the work began. In early May the first iron was laid and a needle switch installed at the junction with the main line. At the same time crews began stringing telephone wire on the branch and on the main.[3] Unlike most railroads, the Catskill lines never used the telegraph, but relied on timetable operation, later supplemented by phone orders. By June a water tank, two sidings and a 25′ x 60′ station were under construction at Cairo. Workmen were installing a turntable at Cairo Junction, apparently anticipating semi-independent operation of the branch, whereby regular Catskill Mountain trains would pick up cars at this point.[4] That this was the original plan is strengthened by the delivery later of the first locomotive, numbered "1" and lettered "Cairo Railroad." In a few years this traffic arrangement was modified, the turntable was removed and the engine renumbered as No. 3 of the Catskill Mountain Railroad. And despite a rearrangement of executives, the same men appeared as directors for the Cairo — C. L. Beach, A. Van Santvoord, C. L. Rickerson and others. The little railroad "system" out of Catskill was under tight control of the powerful river and resort interests.

But that the Catskill route no longer had a railroad monopoly was now evident. The Ulster & Delaware-sponsored narrow gauge line up the Stony Clove had spawned its own branch, the 7½-mile Kaaterskill Railroad. This meant that New York City residents could travel by rail almost the entire distance to the heart of the Catskill resort country. At either end a short gap had to be bridged by other means, but the trip from the metropolis to the Catskill Mountain House had become more direct and more convenient. The Catskill vacationer could cross on a ferry to the

Stony Clove & Catskill Mountain mogul. The S. C. & M. line to Hunter posed an immediate threat to the Catskill Mountain, a threat carried out by the construction of the narrow gauge link from its line to the Hotel Kaaterskill. (*Edward P. Baumgardner Collection*)

New Jersey terminal of the New York, West Shore & Buffalo, journeying then by rail to within a mile of Charles Beach's hotel. Two changes of cars were still necessary, at Kingston to a waiting U. & D. train and at Phoenicia to the Stony Clove's narrow gauge equipage. At Kaaterskill station the train stopped, just short of the Mountain House property. Here, however, stood the spanking new (1881) Hotel Kaaterskill, set high and ostentatious atop South Mountain. When the rails reached this spot, the U. & D. management and the Hotel Kaaterskill's owner, George Harding, believed that they had built an alternate route preferable to the steamboat-rail-stagecoach jaunt imposed upon vacationers using the Catskill entry to the mountains. They had not reckoned with the inventiveness of their competitors.

After a reorganization of the Catskill Mountain Railroad as the Catskill Mountain *Railway* in June (in which Alfred Van Santvoord became president and C. L. Beach vice-president), the

investors determined to scale the steep Wall of Manitou in order to reach the Mountain House and its neighboring hotels. So, in November of 1885, they filed articles of association for the Otis Elevating Railway. The plan was to lift passengers by cable car between the base and the summit of the mountains, where connection would be made with the more conventional railway. The Otis Elevator Company, a firm specializing in such construction, was called into consultation and a survey was run in 1887.[5]

But the construction was not begun immediately. For several years the management concentrated on the railroad they already had. A gratifying increase in patronage during June, July and August did not compensate for the falling off of business during the winter. The Cairo branch had been a disappointment, in this respect. Some passengers even boycotted the trains because of the 10¢ a mile fare imposed on Cairo customers. The charge was eventually reduced and the Catskill

54

The old station at Cairo. Shortly after construction of the Cairo branch, this frame structure served for both freight and passengers. Within a few years, a new passenger depot would be erected and this building used only for freight. *(William Bissinger Collection)*

The Kaaterskill's DERRICK VAN BRUMMEL. When this locomotive began its passenger hauls in 1883, the summer boarder could travel by rail from New York City to the Catskills. *(Thomas Norrell Collection)*

Catskill Mountain Railway first-income bond. Issued to Charles L. Beach, this $500 certificate was the first sold in 1885. (Greene County Historical Society)

The Kaaterskill's RIP VAN WINKLE. While "baggage smashers" attend to front-end business, the train crew assumes the traditional stance for their portrait. (*Karl Korbel Collection*)

company leased the branch, including its new Dickson locomotive, for $2,700 a year.[6]

Substantial improvements were made to the railroad property during these early years. The roadbed received new ballast and new ties, the trestlework under the three tracks at the Point was filled and grade and alignment changes were made. During the years 1885 through 1891, the biennial state inspections found consistently that general maintenance was satisfactory and that the motive power was "in exceedingly good condition," a tribute to John L. Driscoll and his engineers, who overhauled the locomotives each winter.[7] The cars, which stood exposed to the elements all year long, showed the effects and their appearance (but not *condition*) was often criticized by the inspectors. From December to May each year, the coaches, cars and engines stood idle until the summer visitors reappeared.

In preparation for the throngs in 1892, the company finally went ahead with plans for the Otis. In January of 1892 the Board of Railroad Commis-

sioners granted the Otis directors' application for an increase in capital stock from $100,000 to $170,-000, with the assurance that the road would be in operation on or about July 1st. The contracts were then let: to Pennel and Obern for grading and masonry, to Charles Bucki for timber work and to Otis Brothers for the iron work. As might be expected, Charles L. Beach donated Mountain House land for the purpose and his nephew, Charles A. Beach, purchased the remaining right-of-way, a hundred-foot swath up the mountainside. Crews of southern Negroes were soon blasting and cutting their way upwards on the steep slopes.[8] The way would soon be clear to the Mountain House by rail. But there remained that rail-less gap between there and Kaaterskill station, the one-mile link for vacationers bound for other hotels along "Resort Ridge," the seven-mile hotel-studded stretch between the Mountain House and Tannersville.

The Ulster & Delaware's subsidiary, Kaaterskill Railroad, had no intention of making the Cats-

The Cairo train at the Landing, about 1890. The first two men, from the left, are Frank Ruf and Martin Brewer, engineer and conductor. *(Alan Ruf Collection)*

Advertisement from *Van Loan's Catskill Mountain Guide.*

58

Construction at the Summit. The station, below, takes shape with cable drums in place and control tower framed in. *(Carl Collection)*

The first station at Otis Junction. In 1893, the Otis met the Catskill Mountain trains but made no rail connection, a situation remedied later. *(Carl Collection)*

The long trestle. Near the base of the mountain the incline crossed Bogart Road over an extensive timber framework. *(Carl Collection)*

Another view of the Otis Summit depot a-building. Here can be seen clearly the three-rail track and the simple mechanical arrangements for raising cars. *(Carl Collection)*

kill route more attractive, for it wanted its Kingston-Phoenicia-Kaaterskill route to prosper. Therefore, it refused to lay another rail in the direction of the Otis. The Catskill-Otis amalgam countered with an angry proposal to build the Catskill & Tannersville Railroad parallel to the Kaaterskill.[9] Van Santvoord and Beach won their point, for the Kaaterskill capitulated. If the C. & T. would lay the one mile of track, the Kaaterskill would furnish the service. An agreement was signed with President Edward Young on November 24th, 1892 "to prevent paralleling the Kaaterskill Road."[10] The transportation gap had been bridged.

The engineer's certificate for provisional acceptance of the Otis Elevating Railroad was signed by Thomas E. Brown on August 3rd, about a month past the deadline. The Fourth of July crowds had come, gazed longingly at the nearly finished Otis from their rocking stagecoaches on the road up the mountain, and gone. But the line would be open for the next season and would undoubtedly draw customers, some just for the novelty of the ride.

The new station for the Mountain House and the mountain top was located about a mile north of Palenville and the same distance south of the old Mountain House station, which was at the old stage road. Passengers could step off the train onto the covered platform at the new Otis Station, which met the Catskill Mountain Railroad at a

OTIS ELEVATING RY.

From Base to Summit of the Catskill Mountains

IN TEN MINUTES.

TIME TABLE NO. 1. TAKES EFFECT MONDAY, JULY , 1892.

NO 15	NO. 11	NO 9	NO. 5	NO 1		N° 4	NO 8	NO 10	NO 14	Sundays Only
P M	P M	P M	A M	A M	*Arrive.* *Leave.*	A M	A M	P M	P M	P M
7.57	4.25	1.20	9.22	6.50	Catskill Mountain Station	7.00	9.50	1.25	4.55	8.50
7.47	4.13	1.10	9.12	6.40	*Leave.* Otis Junction *Arrive.*	7.10	10.05	1.40	5.10	9.05
FROM CATSKILL					CONNECTIONS	TO CATSKILL				
Otis Ry. Evening Special.	Day Line Otis Ry. Special.	N. Y. and Otis Ry. Special.	Otis Ry. Mountain Excursion	NightLine Otis Ry. Special.	*VIA* Catskill Mtn. Ry.	New York Morning Express.	Otis Ry. Day Line & RR. Ex.	Afternoon Express.	Otis Ry. NightLine & RR. Ex.	Steamer Kaatersk'l Special.
Sundays also.			Sundays also.	Sundays also.		Sundays also.			Sundays also.	July 10 to Aug 28
7.15	3.40		8.38	6.08	West Shore Station	7.46	10.41	2.16	5.46	9.45
7.05	3.35	12.35	8.35	6.05	Catskill Village	7.50	10.45	2.20	5.50	9.50
7.00	3.30	12.30	8.30	6.00	Catskill Landing	7.55	10.50	2.25	5.55	9.55
P M	P M	Noon.	A M	A M		A M	A M	P M	P M	P M
FROM NEW YORK					VIA	TO NEW YORK				
				P M					A M	A M
	A M			6.00	Catskill Line Steamers		P M		5.00	5.00
P M	9.00		Leave Albany		H. R. Day Line Steamers		5.30		P M	
3.30	11.30	9.20	7.15		N. Y. C. & H. R. RR.	11.20	2.10	6.41	9.20	
3.45	11.35	*			West Shore Railroad		2.50	5.55	9·55	
P M	A M	A M	A M	P M	*Leave.* *Arrive.*	A M	P M	P M	P M	A M

*** From New York to the Summit of the Catskills in Four Hours.**

The Otis Ry. cars will also run at other hours for the accommodation of excursion parties.

Supt.

Printer's proof of the first Otis timetable. Notice that the effective date in July is blank, as is the space for the superintendent's name. This item comes from the collection of Mr. and Mrs. C. A. W. Beach. Mr. Beach is the son of Charles Addison Beach.

OTIS ELEVATING RAILWAY.

From Base to Summit of the Catskill Mountains in Ten Minutes.

TIME-TABLE NO. 1. TAKES EFFECT THURSDAY, AUG. 4, 1892.

No *15	No. 11	No. 9	No.* 5	No.* 1		No.* 4	No. 8	No. 10	No. *14	S'nd'y only.
P M	P M	P M	A M	A M	*Arrive.* *Leave.*	A M	A M	P M	P M	P M
7.57	4.25	1.20	9.22	6.50	Catskill Mountain Station.	7.00	9.50	1.25	4.55	8.50
7.47	4.13	1.10	9.12	6.40	*Lv.*... Otis Junction ... *Ar.*	7.10	10.05	1.40	5.10	9.05
FROM CATSKILL.					CONNECTIONS.	TO CATSKILL.				
					VIA CATSKILL MTN. RY.					
7.15	3.40		8.38	6.08	.... West Shore Station.....	7.46	10.41	2.16	5.46	9.45
7.05	3.35	12.35	8.35	6.05	.... Catskill Village.......	7.50	10.45	2.20	5.50	9.50
7.00	3.30	12.30	8.30	6.00	.... Catskill Landing......	7.55	10.50	2.25	5.55	9.55
P M	P M	Noon	A M	A M		A M	A M	P M	P M	P M
FROM NEW YORK.					VIA	TO NEW YORK.				
				P M					A M	A M
	A M		Leave	6.00	...Catskill Line Steamers..		P M		5.00	5.00
P M	9.00		Alb'ny		.H. R. Day Line Steamers.		5.30		P M	
3.30	11.30	9.20	7.15		...N. Y. C. & H. R. RR....	11.20	2.10	6.41	9.20	
3.45	11.35				.... West Shore Railroad...		2.50	5.55	9.55	
P M	A M	A M	A M	P M	*Leave.* *Arrive.*	A M	P M	P M	P M	A M

Sundays only to and including Aug. 28th.

From New York to the Summit of the Catskills in Four Hours.

* Trains 1, 5, 15, 4 and 14 Run on Sundays also.

The Otis Ry. cars will also run at other hours for the accommodation of excursion parties.

CHAS. A. BEACH, Supt., Catskill, N. Y.

A pocket timetable. The July date has been altered to August 4, 1892 on this schedule.

Cairo yard. This later photo shows the new station at left. (*Winfield W. Robinson Collection at Colgate University*)

The new engine, below, at Cairo. First No. 4 was broken in on the Cairo run after her arrival from Schenectady. (*Alan Ruf Collection*)

No. 2 at Cairo. At rest but sighing contentedly through the safety valve, the MANN has just been turned on the gallows-type turntable just visible at far left center. *(Charles Cammer Collection)*

right angle. The Otis itself was 7,000 feet long, raising its patrons 1600 feet up the mountainside. The track was laid with three rails, each car using an outer and the inner rail. At the halfway point this middle rail branched out and became two rails, so that there was a double track at the turnout. The cars passed here and continued on the three-rail track above and below this meeting place. Each train had a passenger car seating 75 persons and a baggage car. As was the custom, the cars were named —"Rickerson" and "Van Santvoord." Inside they had strong stationary seats of chestnut slats with curved backs, and outside they were painted a wine color. A brakeman was provided on each train, as a safety measure.[11]

Safety was also provided for in an automatic emergency brake. Two cables were attached to the passenger car by means of a pivoted metal plate which would turn and activate a safety grip if speed became excessive. The teeth on the grip would dig into the wooden guard rail and stop the car. Thus, the passengers were doubly protected; brakes could be set by the trainman or by the automatic mechanical device. And the power hoist at Otis Summit was more than adequate to do the work. Two Hamilton Corliss engines drove two Walker differential drums (twelve feet in diameter) which were placed in tandem. Around these drums were wound 1¼" cables 7500 feet long, having a tensile strength of 104 tons. Around these drums were strap brakes operated by air pressure from a Westinghouse air pump. The cable drums and engines occupied part of the Otis Summit station, atop which perched the operator's tower,

65

Advertisement from *Van Loan's Catskill Mountain Guide.*

A slight mishap on the C. & T. An overturned horse-drawn roller caused a temporary delay in grading this one-mile railroad from the Summit to Kaaterskill Station. *(Carl Collection)*

holding the levers for controlling the ascent and descent of cars. In his isolated splendor, the tower-man resembled the skipper on a Hudson River steamer, but earthbound and without a wheel in his "wheelhouse." Opposite the station-engine room, the powerhouse was set and the steam generated there flowed through large wrapped pipes to the 12″ x 30″ cylinders.[12]

On August 4th, the Otis began operating trains up the rugged mountainside, through four deep rock cuts and over three timber trestles, one 72 feet high. When the conductor of the train at the Otis Junction station gave the "All aboard!" he then signaled the Otis Summit towerman by pressing a bell button in the station. At the ringing of the bell, the towerman threw the lever engaging the cable drums in the room below him. As one drum began revolving slowly to take up the cable attached to this lower car, the other drum turned in the opposite direction, paying out cable to lower the upper car. In addition to the simple bell signal,

each passenger car contained a telephone connected to the tower, so that the towerman could be notified of trouble when the cars were out of sight or earshot. Nothing seemed lacking for the safety and convenience of patrons.

Now, for 75¢, passengers could save more than an hour of travel time and simultaneously enjoy an incomparable view of the Hudson Valley below and the mountains above, on their way to their favored resort accommodations in the Catskill range. Since the stage fare had been $1.25 plus 50¢ per trunk, the Otis was almost overwhelmingly attractive to summer visitors. All in all, the prospects for the Catskill Mountain, Cairo and Otis lines seemed bright.

Meanwhile, as powerful business interests pushed track up onto and over the promontories, others were convinced that something could be made of the level route beyond Cairo. In 1890, C. Bennett ran a survey for the Catskill, Middleburgh and Cooperstown Rail Road, following the Cana-

67

Construction at the Summit. The power house smokestack has been erected and a cribbed-up Otis baggage car can be seen just to the right of it. *(Carl Collection)*

joharie roadbed (constructed and projected) as far as Middleburgh. Despite opposition from Cairo businessmen, who saw a distinct advantage in having rail receivers and shippers come into their village, the project was kept alive for at least two years. During its paper life, the C., M. & C. merged with the equally intangible South Cairo & East Durham.[13] Despite this and other proposals to send railroad trains up the Catskill valley, the established route from Catskill to Cairo and Palenville remained the only substance to the dream.

More practical men had completed a railroad system, in miniature, that would service area interests very well. The unity of control made for cer-

tain economies of operation, including the establishment of a common office upstairs in the Catskill village station for the management of the Catskill Mountain, Otis Elevating and the newly formed Catskill & Tannersville. The last link in the railroad chain, just one mile in length, took shape when Moirs and Lewis accepted the construction contract and C. F. Parker accepted the task of engineering the route. Men and teams arrived on December 1 aboard the *Catskill*.[14] Soon after the Catskill Mountain Railway discontinued its schedule for the winter.

In preparation for a new season, the Catskill Mountain Railway ordered two boxcars and two

68

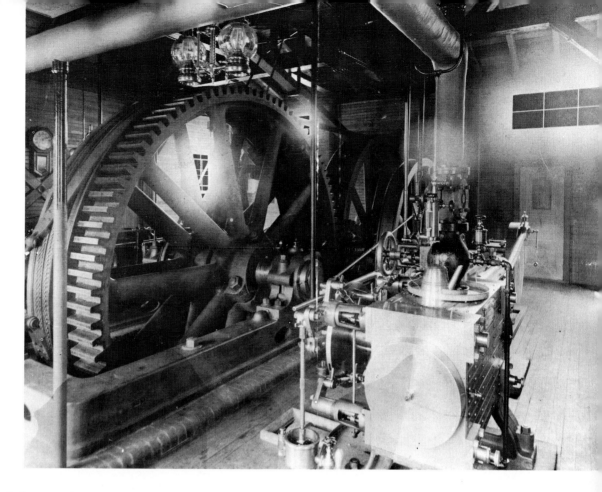

The completed station, below, at Otis Summit. Passengers could walk up the ramp, down the stairs and onto a waiting train of a more conventional type. The steam pipe from the power house is clearly visible here. *(Carl Collection)*

A closer view of the Otis cable drums. Here was the control center for the entire elevating operation. *(Author's Collection)*

At the turnout. This 1892 photo, above, catches two Otis trains passing midway on the line. *(Carl Collection)*

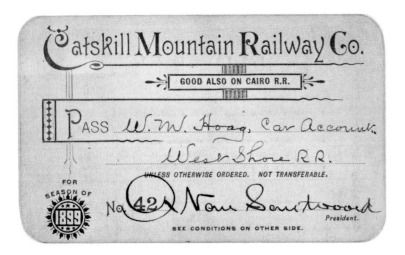

coaches from the Jackson & Sharp Company of Wilmington, Delaware. These arrived in early July and found immediate use. Not only were passenger revenues up, but traffic to Cairo was increasing. The Cairo station, with its awkward high platform and poor location among sidings, was turned into a freight house; a new passenger station began to take form. The turntable at Cairo Junction was pulled out and a wye installed for the better dispatch of trains.[15] In order to stimulate additional travel, the company announced in the local newspapers that it would reduce rates to $2 for the round trip between Catskill and Otis Station. The influx was expected to be greater than ever.

The 1890 census for Greene County showed that the summer population more than doubled (from 31,000 to 70,000) the winter population in more than 900 boarding houses. What had once been the province of the black bear and the catamount was now the playground for vacationing humanity. In a time when merchants for patent medicine advised that their concoctions would cure consumption, warts, chills, fever, cancer, loss of appetite and general debility (either singly or collectively), it was surely no great exaggeration to sing the praises of the rarefied atmosphere of the Catskills, which would furnish

> more life for the body, increased energy for the stomach, new incentives of mind — this is the gospel you learn on the Catskill Mountains. Here you will find the elixir which will make you youthful and useful and untiring.[16]

If that were the gospel, then *Van Loan's Catskill Mountain Guide,* the annually published compendium of Catskilliana, was the bible. Followers of the "religion" crowded into this great outdoor meetinghouse more easily now that there were railroad tracks through the very heart of the mountains.

The Ulster & Delaware Railroad absorbed (by 999-year lease) the Stony Clove & Catskill Mountain, as well as the Kaaterskill, into its system in 1893. This move demonstrated confidence that these slim gauge railroads could make money for the parent company. And State Railroad Inspector F. K. Baxter found similar confidence on the part of the Catskill company, for "considerable improvement has been made since last inspection" although his ride was not entirely comfortable. The sharply winding track through Austin's Glen, a bugaboo for the Canajoharie road also, led to a "shock upon taking curves and leaving them [which] is not gentle." At these points he noted much worn rail and replacements of curved rail with straight sections, a practice leading to a whip-cracking sensation as the little trains surged into the turns.[17]

In spite of the difficulties of terrain, the Catskill lines had penetrated the lucrative resort territory with the bold thrust of steel rails. Not only had the Catskill Mountain Railway approached the foot of the precipice but the Otis had actually scaled the Wall of Manitou. This was perhaps the most audacious of achievements. It was, as the *Recorder* said, "a slide fit for Titans."[18]

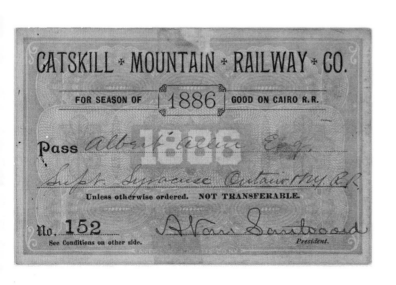

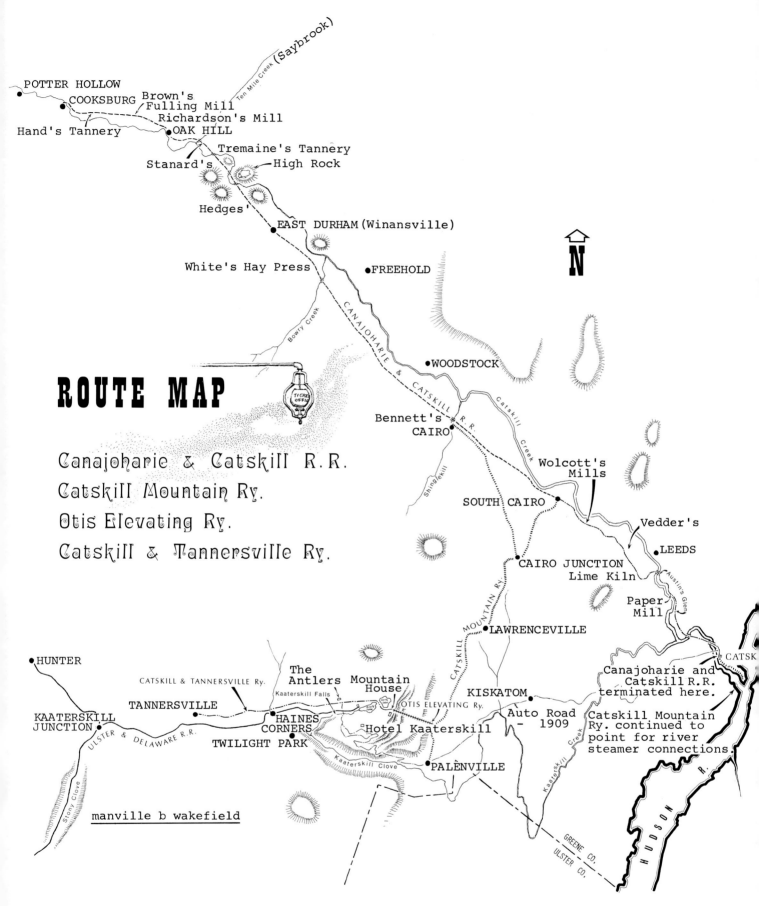

ROUTE MAP

Canajoharie & Catskill R.R.
Catskill Mountain Ry.
Otis Elevating Ry.
Catskill & Tannersville Ry.

POTTER HOLLOW
COOKSBURG
Brown's
Fulling Mill
Hand's Tannery
Richardson's Mill
OAK HILL
Tremaine's Tannery
Stanard's
High Rock
Hedges'
EAST DURHAM (Winansville)
White's Hay Press
FREEHOLD
Ten Mile Creek (Saybrook)
Bowry Creek
CANAJOHARIE & CATSKILL R.R.
WOODSTOCK
Catskill Creek
Bennett's
CAIRO
Wolcott's Mills
SOUTH CAIRO
Vedder's
Shinglekill
CAIRO JUNCTION
Lime Kiln
LEEDS
Austin's Glen
Paper Mill
CATSKILL MOUNTAIN Ry.
LAWRENCEVILLE

HUNTER
CATSKILL & TANNERSVILLE Ry.
TANNERSVILLE
Kaaterskill Falls
The Antlers Mountain House
KISKATOM
CATSK
Canajoharie and Catskill R.R. terminated here.
KAATERSKILL JUNCTION
ULSTER & DELAWARE R.R.
HAINES CORNERS
OTIS ELEVATING Ry.
Hotel Kaaterskill
Auto Road 1909
Catskill Mountain Ry. continued to point for river steamer connections.
TWILIGHT PARK
Kaaterskill Clove
Story Clove
PALENVILLE
Kaaterskill Creek
GREENE CO.
ULSTER CO.
HUDSON R.

manville b wakefield

CHAPTER EIGHT

Gains and Losses

AN EVENT taking place in another corner of New York State was to have a profound effect upon the fortunes of the Catskill Mountain Railway. In 1888 the Elmira Shale Brick Company successfully produced a new kind of brick, tough and hard but not brittle like common brick. As the company name implies, the process used the harder stony deposits rather than the soft plastic clays of common or "mud" brick. The qualities of strength and durability made shale brick admirably suited for pavement of highways and streets. The demand grew. Within a few years shale brick plants would be located at Binghamton, Corning, Olean, Hornell, Jamestown, Newfield and Syracuse, as well as at Elmira. Brick, a cheap and bulky product, required inexpensive transportation which none of these locations had. All of these operations depended entirely upon relatively costly railroad freight to get the product to market.[1]

Brickyards, of course, already lined the banks of the Hudson River below Catskill, enjoying the advantage of the low cost transportation of the brick barge. If a large quantity of shale could be found near the Hudson shore, the production of shale brick at the water's edge could prove highly profitable. Such a deposit, of red Chemung shale, did exist, near Cairo, on the branch leased by the Catskill Mountain Railway Company. Even closer to the village were banks of clay suitable for ordinary building brick and for the shale brick mixture.

By 1894 the Catskill Shale Brick Company had been formed and property purchased along the creek and on the railroad line. The land cleared, situated near to the Canajoharie & Catskill's termination point, eliminated a landmark known as the "Stone Jug" or "Dies' Folly." This gray stone mansion had been built by Major John Dies in Revolutionary times when he is said to have deserted the British Army. In the excitement over the new local industry, no regret was felt locally for its destruction.

Even before the kilns were in operation, Shale Brick and the Railway had worked out their agreement. By it, Shale Brick agreed to buy and maintain dump cars for carrying shale rock; the Railway was required to build the needed sidings at the new plant and at Cairo. The freight charges would be 50¢ a ton base for each month and 25¢ a ton if the tonnage exceeded 5,000 in any one month. The increased income would be welcome to the railroad, even though it would mean investment in more motive power. Now the railroad would be running three locomotives regularly — the scheduled mixed trains to Cairo and to Palenville, plus the shale train. Just three locomotives were on the roster; there would be no engine in reserve. To remedy this lack, the directors approved the purchase of a new and heavier locomotive, to be named the CHARLES L. BEACH. Delivered in 1895 from Schenectady, No. 4 found steady employment. Due to increased orders, Catskill Shale Brick soon increased its production from 100,000 to 150,000 paving bricks a day.[2]

Even with the added locomotive, other adjustments had to be made. A third crew would be put on to run the shale train. The members of the original crew cannot be ascertained, but in 1897 they were Burr Vaughn, conductor; Charles Long, engineer; Lewis Freese, fireman; George Richter and William Duston, brakemen.[3] And because the company did not operate freight trains, some sort of caboose or crew car would have to be provided for these men. Passenger coaches and baggage cars being in constant use during the summer, a

73

Loading clay near Catskill. Man-made erosion has cut back the bank to feed the brick kilns. *(Winfield W. Robinson Collection at Colgate University)*

boxcar was rebuilt with windows and end doors. No cupola would be needed since the low shale cars would not obstruct the view from the caboose. Solid trains of shale were soon arriving at the unloading trestle at the Catskill plant just below East Main Street. Flying dust from the dumping operation brought so many complaints from nearby residents that Shale Brick enclosed the area in canvas.[4]

By 1898 shale and clay accounted for 70,545 tons of the 74,407 total tons of freight hauled by the Catskill Mountain Railway.[5] For the most part, other freight was for reshipment by steamer from Catskill to New York City or from the West Shore to the most distant points on the Catskill Mountain line. There could be no interchange of cars with this trunk line from New York to Buffalo, of course. Not only was the Catskill equipment narrow gauge, but the West Shore line soared high above Catskill Creek and the local railway on a

long trestle. There was no connection. Passengers did sometimes transfer from the West Shore to the Catskill Mountain trains below, but this meant either a short omnibus trip or a long walk. For these travelers, the railway had erected a small depot under the trestle, giving the village three stations maintained by the same company, a distinction few large cities could boast of.[6] For many summer visitors, the route by way of the West Shore to Kingston, then to Kaaterskill on the Ulster & Delaware must have seemed more direct. The Ulster & Delaware eliminated the change of trains at Phoenicia when it standard gauged the lines up the Clove to Kaaterskill station, an added attraction.[7] But this would cause difficulties for the one-mile narrow gauge Catskill & Tannersville.

Actually, trouble between the Catskill & Tannersville and the Kaaterskill roads had begun as early as 1894 when, contrary to the operating agreement, the Kaaterskill cut its fares. This re-

74

One of the first shale trains. No. 2 and its consist of ten cars stopped at the third bridge for a photograph. At the end of the train is the cupola-less caboose. *(George Phelps Collection)*

No. 4 just after delivery. The CHARLES L. BEACH was soon assigned to the shale run. Below engineer Charles Long and fireman Fred Prediger assume a familiar pose. *(Winfield W. Robinson Collection at Colgate University)*

Kaaterskill Station. After standard gauging, the branch from Phoenicia offered strong competition to the narrow gauge lines from Catskill.
(*Library of Congress*)

The Hotel Kaaterskill. George Harding's great hostelry overshadowed (almost literally) the Catskill Mountain House. *(Library of Congress)*

U. & D. No. 21 on the old Kaaterskill line. Vacationers were attracted to the rivals of the Catskill lines by the directness of the Ulster & Delaware route to the mountain tops. *(Library of Congress)*

---

duced the C. & T.'s share of earnings and simultaneously made the Kingston entry to the mountains more economical to travelers. A new contract in 1895 stipulated that the Kaaterskill would run four special trains a day between Otis Summit and Tannersville at a cost to the C. & T. of $24 a day. Service was erratic, however, and the contract was terminated by mutual agreement in 1897. Moreover, President Coykendall of the Ulster & Delaware did not wish to reopen the discussions. Under the circumstances, the Catskill company had little choice but to extend the road, as first planned, to Tannersville. In a letter to Superintendent Charles A. Beach, dated January 29, 1898, Commodore Van Santvoord confirmed this view:

> If it cannot be built in time [for the 1898 summer season] we are in a very bad shape. With-

78

out a connection to the Otis, it will be of no use to run the incline, and the loss of traffic of the Catskill Mountain Railway will be diminished to the extent of at least $8,000.

For a railroad earning only about $2,000 a year above expenses, this would be disastrous. Casting about for ways and means, Van Santvoord, Beach and Master Mechanic Driscoll considered gasoline motor cars and then settled on used equipment — steam locomotives and cars.

Makeshift arrangements were apparently concluded with the Kaaterskill for the 1898 season, after which the U. & D. subsidiary began its gauge change. In 1899, the Catskill & Tannersville began to live up to its name. The first construction was from Kaaterskill station to Haines Corners, a distance of about four miles. By August 15th the last segment had been completed, for a total distance of about five and a half miles, and regular service began. The State Inspector, however, found much to criticize and little to praise. A portion of his report makes frightening reading:

> The road, even when completed as designed, will be poorly adapted for operation as a steam road. The curves are very frequent and sharp (up to 20 degrees), the grades are very heavy (264 feet per mile), with frequent and abrupt changes. The line and surfacing of track are very poor, curves are irregular in line and surface, and in some places the outer is lower than the inner rail. . . . One derailment has already occurred, and with the track in present condition others are likely to occur at any time.

Questioning the company's right to operate trains at all, he suggested a maximum speed of 8 (eight) miles per hour.[8] Haste and economy had caused many of the defects noted, but there was another factor. The line that followed the difficult topography best was already in the possession of the Kaaterskill branch of the Ulster & Delaware.

Even after ditches had been dug, rails had been aligned, embankments had been strengthened, ballast had been added and curves had been properly graded, the Catskill & Tannersville remained a second-class railroad property. The tree-lined right-of-way (branches of which sometimes brushed along the car tops) twisted and turned along the slopes, constantly climbing or coasting. The curves and grades could not be improved, although by 1901 the timetable called for a speed double that recommended by the 1899 inspection report — 16 miles per hour.

The leisurely pace of these trains and the willingness of their crews to stop anywhere earned the railroad an affectionate nickname. For local residents and regular visitors it became "The Huckleberry," a fruit which abounded along the line.[9] During the berry season, passengers and railroaders became berry pickers. And when the crews could not, in good conscience, allow their schedule to be ignored completely, they could be "bribed" with a basket or two to make an unscheduled pickup of pickers on their return trip. More than any other railroad in the vicinity — the Otis, the Kaaterskill or the Catskill Mountain — the "Huckleberry" was a people's railroad.

Its connection, the Otis Elevating, was reorganized in 1899 and became simply "The Otis."[10] Why "Elevating" was dropped from the corporate nomenclature is difficult to assess. Perhaps the managers wished to de-emphasize the suggestion of dizzying height or to minimize the prospect of a change of trains at Otis Junction. For the Ulster & Delaware was now able to offer through train service from Kingston to Hotel Kaaterskill. That this route offered stiff competition is illustrated by the annual railroad reports for 1900. The Kaaterskill carried 30,000 passengers, the Huckleberry 11,000. The Catskill company must have felt like the man who had to run fast in order not to lose ground.

The Catskill & Tannersville's deficit (almost $2,000 for 1900) was as nothing compared to other losses suffered by all the Catskill lines in the next two years. On July 20, 1901, at the age of 82, Commodore Alfred Van Santvoord died. Appropriately enough, he was aboard his yacht the *Clermont* when the attack came, and the Day Line's *City of Albany* carried the steamboat king to Albany for burial.[11] Then, at 12 noon on October 2, 1902, Charles L. Beach, the grand old man of the Catskills passed away at the age of 94 years[12] His name had become synonymous with the resort business. Both men had been instrumental in the formation and operation of the Catskill Mountain, Otis, and Catskill & Tannersville enterprises. Though the railroads had been marginal carriers, they had served the hotels and steamboats well. Beach and Van Santvoord had been strong supporters of the little system.

Their loss would be felt.

A view down the Otis. The Hudson winds majestically across the top of this photo as an Otis train descends to the old station. *(Author's Collection)*

CHAPTER NINE

Good Years

ALFRED VAN SANTVOORD and Charles L. Beach did not live to see some of the best years the little railroads would ever have. In the five-year period between 1899 and 1903, there had been a dramatic upturn in passenger traffic. The statistics[1] tell the story:

	1899	1903
Catskill Mountain Ry.	22,000	57,000
Otis Ry.	14,000	25,000
Catskill & Tannersville Ry.	18,000	37,000
Total	54,000	119,000

Summer visitors continued to throng the decks of Hudson River sidewheelers, to ride the slim rails of the Catskill Mountain Railway, to board the cable cars at Otis Junction and then, at the Summit, to either check in at the famous Mountain House or board the Huckleberry for a short trip farther on.

To cope with this growing passenger load, the Catskill Evening Line had commissioned a new steamer, the *Onteora,* the first steel-hulled liner constructed for the company. Built at the Marvel Shipyard at Newburgh, the *Onteora* joined the *Kaaterskill* on the New York to Catskill run. According to her designer, J. W. Millard, he made only one miscalculation about her performance — she was much faster than he expected her to be. Now, for the dollar fare, the Catskills-bound excursionist could take the *Onteora* at 1:30 p.m. or the *Kaaterskill* at 6 p.m. on any Saturday during the season. On weekdays only a single trip was made, the two boats alternating on this duty. The "shortest, cheapest and best route" as both the steamboat and railroad advertisements boasted, was enjoying an enviable passenger traffic.[2]

For the Evening Line, the large new sidewheeler answered the need for improved facilities; for the little railroads, the solution was not so easy.

Wear and tear on the track and structures now became a serious problem, especially for the Otis, which maintained extensive wooden trestlework. Approximately one-third of the route was supported in this fashion. Timber renewal was a constant chore.

Another time-consuming task for Otis employees was the transfer of Catskill Mountain House provisions and Otis powerhouse coal from Catskill Mountain Railway cars to the Otis baggage "trailers." Some ease of handling could be accomplished, of course, by routing this freight traffic over the rival Kaaterskill line, but this would deprive the town of Catskill and its railroads of the business. No serious thought was ever given to such a treasonable action.

Instead, in 1903 and 1904, the Otis Company reconstructed its line at a cost of almost $27,000. The work eliminated 1,700 feet of trestle and reduced the mileage from 1.35 to 1.08 miles. This lowering and truncation of the line had two distinct advantages: it reduced maintenance costs and enabled the railroad to transfer cars from the Catskill to the Otis. The station at Otis Junction was moved back from its former location to a point closer to Bogart Road (which now had an underpass rather than the previous overpass). Then crews built a wye, one leg of which struck towards Palenville, the other towards Catskill. Passenger trains from Catskill now headed into the Otis station on one leg and backed out on to the main line for the short run into Palenville. At the mountain top the Catskill & Tannersville laid a connecting track for switching of cars from the Otis to their line. The use of the slant-seated Otis cars was still necessary for passengers, but freight cars could now be coupled to the cable cars for the trip up the incline.[3]

The *Onteora*, as built. Sleek and handsome, the newest Catskill night boat bore some resemblance to an ocean liner. *(Steamship Historical Society of America, Inc.)*

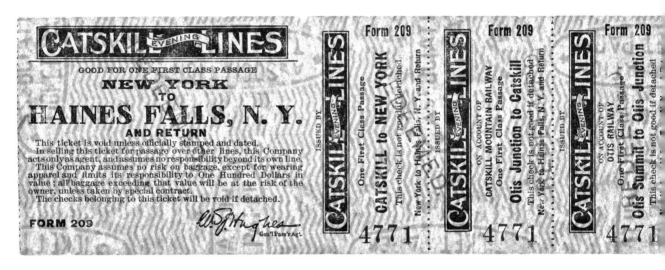

The long trestle. Another Ruf photograph exhibits the elaborate timber structure at the base of the Otis. The sign reads "All persons forbidden walking on trussel." *(Winfield W. Robinson Collection at Colgate University)*

After the Otis reconstruction. When the wooden bridging was removed, a cut was made, the road was underpassed and the station was moved closer to the mountains. (*S. Elmer Davis photo from the collection of Barbara Rivette.*)

For this purpose, four small cars of 5-ton capacity took shape at the railroad shop at the Landing. These proved so useful that a duplicate order was soon completed. Eventually, 4 gondolas and 4 boxcars entered interchange service between the Catskill Mountain, Otis and Catskill & Tannersville lines.[4] Between Catskill Landing and Tannersville, freight could now travel without reloading. Even though passengers could not enjoy the same privilege, one obstacle on the route had been eliminated. John L. Driscoll, described by former employees as "that bright Englishman," is credited with the plan and its execution.

Envy of the Otis's success inspired at least one rival scheme to climb the mountain wall from the base. In March of 1904, the Albany *Times-Union*

reported that one George H. Kemp intended to build an "airship railway" from Palenville up the Kaaterskill Clove to Haines Corners. A gas bag would be filled at Palenville Station and the car would ascend the heights guided by two steel cables. At the summit, the gas would be pumped out and returned through a pipe to Palenville. The descent would be by the use of "aeroplanes" (no further explanation) and with the braking power of a light hoisting engine at Haines Corners.[5] Needless to say, the "airship railroad" was never built. The Otis retained its unique function.

One Catskill traveler who recalls the exhilarating Otis experience is T. J. Sheehey, now of Montclair, New Jersey:

83

Running on the new line. From another vantage point the Otis train can be seen entering the short new excavation under the highway. A horse-drawn dumpcart stands at the end of the platform. *(S. Elmer Davis photo from the collection of Barbara Rivette)*

I think there were no more than thirty passengers entraining at the Troy (N. Y.) station that August morning for the "Excursion to the Catskills." The year was 1904 and excursions by rail were quite popular; there were very few automobiles and practically no paved highways of any length. It was possible in those early years of the present century to go to New York City from Troy and return on a Sunday excursion for only two dollars. I don't know why the Catskill excursion attracted so few patrons. The Greene County area hadn't reached the fame as a resort region that it has enjoyed the past two or three decades but there were large and elegant hotels such as Catskill Mountain House and Hotel Kaaterskill reached by not one but two railroads.

I am not clear as to why we were routed from Troy to Greendale on the New York Central,— and then by ferry to Catskill Landing,— instead of from Troy to Albany and then via the West Shore R. R. to Catskill village. Perhaps it was

because the excursion car was attached to a regular Troy-New York City train and thus avoided a special on the West Shore. In any case it involved for us the use of at least five transportation services to get to Tannersville, N. Y. (As it happened we actually used six services as will be explained.)

The most impressive sight that I recall on our 1904 excursion was the unfolding of the Hudson Valley and its river as the cable car ascended the mountain from Otis Junction. The map gives the length of the ride as 1.3 miles but of course this was not straight up. However, I should say that we rose perhaps 1500 ft. from the Junction and this naturally laid open to view a vast area, beautiful in the morning sun.

Our tickets carried us to Tannersville and return but when we reached Otis Summit the narrow gauge train was not at hand. We wandered over to the lawn of the Catskill Mountain House (and here was another magnificent view) when we

::Information for Passengers::

Through Tickets For sale via Hudson River Day Line Steamers, Catskill Evening Line Steamers, New York Central Railroad, West Shore Railroad and *connecting lines*, at all Ticket Offices in New York City, Brooklyn, Philadelphia, Boston and other principal cities.

ASK FOR TICKETS VIA CATSKILL AND HAVE BAGGAGE CHECKED TO DESTINATION

Stage Connections From Cairo Stages leave Cairo daily, except Sunday, for Acra, South Durham, East Windham, Union Society, Hensonville, Windham, Ashland and Prattsville at 12 o'clock noon, and for Acra, South Durham, East Windham, Freehold, East Durham, Oak Hill, Durham, Cooksburgh, Preston Hollow and Potter's Hollow at 12 o'clock noon, and 4.30 P. M.

LIVERY IN ATTENDANCE ON ARRIVAL OF ALL TRAINS

AT OTIS JUNCTION, on the Catskill Mountain Railway, connection is made with the OTIS RAILWAY for Catskill Mountain House, Hotel Kaaterskill, Laurel House, Haines Corners and Tannersville.

OTIS SUMMIT, at the summit of the Otis incline railway, is 300 feet from the Catskill Mountain House and one mile from Hotel Kaaterskill. At Otis Summit connection is made by the Catskill and Tannersville Railway for Laurel House, Sunset View, The Antlers, Haines Corners (Twilight, Sunset, Santa Cruz Parks), Tannersville (Onteora and Elka Parks, Schoharie Manor).

Stages from Catskill Mountain House and Hotel Kaaterskill meet passengers at Otis Summit.

PALENVILLE. Stages run to hotels and boarding houses in the vicinity.

Regarding Time Tables This table shows the time trains should arrive at and depart from the several stations and connect with other lines, but their departure, arrival or connection at time stated is not guaranteed.

The time of connecting lines is published for the information of passengers, and every care is taken to keep it correct, but this company does not hold itself responsible for any errors or omissions therein.

DAY LINE SPECIALS — Daily except Sundays. Nos. 6 and 8 connecting with Hudson River Day Line Steamers for New York, and Nos. 11 and 13 connecting with Steamer from New York.

EVENING LINE SPECIALS — Nos. 1 and 3 connecting with Evening Line Steamer from New York, and Nos. 16 and 18 connecting with Steamer for New York. Steamer does not leave Catskill on Saturday or New York on Sunday.

STEAMER ONTEORA SPECIAL — No. 19, Saturdays, only, June 29th to Aug. 31st, inclusive, connecting with Steamer Onteora, leaving New York at 1.30 P. M.

STEAMER KAATERSKILL SPECIALS — Nos. 24 and 26, Sundays only, July 7th to Aug. 25th, inclusive, connecting with Steamer Kaaterskill, leaving Catskill at 10 P. M.

All trains run to or from wharfs of Hudson River Day Line and Catskill Evening Line.

N. Y. CENTRAL SPECIAL — No. 20, Sundays only, connecting with fast N. Y. Central Train leaving Greendale (from Catskill Landing by Ferry) at 5.45 P. M., arriving New York 8.53 P. M.

SPECIAL DELIVERY OF BAGGAGE — Baggage checked at all stations direct to residence, hotel, steamship, ferry, etc., in Greater New York (except the Borough of Richmond), Jersey City, Hoboken, Albany, Troy, Utica, Syracuse, Rochester, Saratoga and Schenectady.

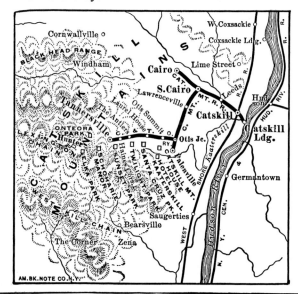

THE ARGUS COMPANY, PRINTERS, ALBANY, N. Y.

The shale train. Loping down Water Street, Number 4 tows a string of shale cars to the kilns. (*A. Fred Saunders Collection*)

Otis Summit through the treetops. This unusual picture taken from the side and at a distance shows the station and power house on one level and the least attractive view of Mountain House just above it. (*Library of Congress*)

86

heard an engine's whistle. Hurrying back, we saw a "solid" Pullman train coming into view on the tracks of the Ulster & Delaware R. R. "Solid" Pullman is a bit of hyperbole; the train consisted of a 4-4-0 engine and *one* chair-car which was empty except for the porter who was pinch-hitting as Pullman conductor. He stepped down from his car (the Catskill & Tannersville and the Ulster & Delaware tracks were adjacent at this point and both within a stone's throw of Catskill Mountain House and Hotel Kaaterskill) and I asked him the destination of his train; he said Tannersville so I said to the other members of our party, "Let's take this." "Oh, it's too expensive," was the response. "What's the fare?" I said turning to the porter. "Twenty-five cents," said he. "Including Pullman?" "That's right." So we got aboard and rode in luxury the whole five miles to Tannersville.[6]

Another passenger, a Mr. H. D. Love, found less to praise about the operation of the trains, especially on the Catskill Mountain segment. On August 17, 1905, he entered a complaint with the Railroad Commissioners about "unsafe" methods of running trains.[7] The specific charge is not stated, but there were at least two possible causes for his action. First of all, the railroad had one notoriously fast engineer, Claude Heath, whose disregard for the winding roadway through Austin's Glen seemed foolhardy. Both Burgett Wolcott and A. W. Phillips recall that members of the train crew sat and braced themselves in the corners of the baggage car when Claude was at the throttle. The speediest runs were on the last trip of the day back to Catskill, whipping into curves and slamming across the three iron bridges. Perhaps Mr. Love had this in mind.

Or, perhaps he was frightened by the flying switch executed by the train crew at the terminus. The maneuver was perfectly legal, as Rule 29 of the railroad regulations specified:

> When approaching Catskill Landing, the speed of all Trains must be greatly reduced before entering Main Street cut. In making the Flying Switch, the signal to disconnect the Train from the Locomotive will be given by the Engineer, after the Train has entered the cut and he has obtained a clear view of the track to the Switches. After the train is cut off from the Locomotive, it must be kept in check in the cut until the Locomotive has passed the Switches and run onto the turn-table track and the signal is given by the Switchman that the switch is properly set for the train to run in on the North Track. The train will then be allowed to run down the grade, by gravity, at a moderate rate of speed, regulated and controlled by the use of the brakes, and only such speed will be allowed as may be necessary to carry the Train to the terminus. When making the Flying Switch, the Conductor and one brakeman must be on the front platform of the first car, and the other Brakeman must be stationed on the rear car, ready to assist in checking the Train on a signal from the Conductor. The utmost care must be used to prevent accidents.[8]

Even if the utmost care *was* used, uninitiated passengers might well wonder where the trainmen had gone (two were hidden from their sight on the platform of the leading baggage car), why the engine had pulled ahead of the train and how they would stop the slowly-moving cars before they plunged into the Hudson. Their nerves were surely not soothed if the crew had also forgotten to detach the bell cord when the engine was uncoupled. Former trainman A. W. Phillips recalls that the breaking of the cord "sounded like a pistol shot" and that it happened "every other time."

While more travelers of both varieties, nervous and tranquil, were swinging up into the narrow-gauge cars, the freight business entered a strange phase. The Catskill Shale Brick Company, promising so much additional revenue to the Catskill Mountain Railway, went bankrupt in 1901. Thus began the bewildering alternations between poverty and prosperity that characterized Shale Brick's operations. In 1899, the company-owned hopper cars carried 98,710 tons of shale and clay, the largest single freight item on the line. In 1905, only 600 tons were loaded.[9] During its insecure existence, the brick kilns underwent two name changes — from Catskill Shale Brick to Eastern Paving Brick to Tidewater Paving Brick — but the new names brought no real change of fortune. And to Catskillians, the smoky, dusty plant was always "Shale Brick." Its impact on village life, for both good and ill, is well remembered. For the railroad management, it was a disappointment.

Another trouble came to the three-railroad system when the Catskill office burned in late winter of 1905, destroying records and correspondence.[10] But, with the past few years' income statements in mind, manager Charles Addison Beach (his title varied through the years but he was the only resident executive) looked forward to better years ahead.

The slim gauge system was a success.

A summer train. No. 1 wheels along with five passenger coaches and baggage car, a sure sign of the summer season. This photo is by W. L. Coursen of Cairo. *(George Phelps Collection)*

Below, a sketch of the Catskill transportation system from *Van Loan's Catskill Mountain Guide* of 1907.

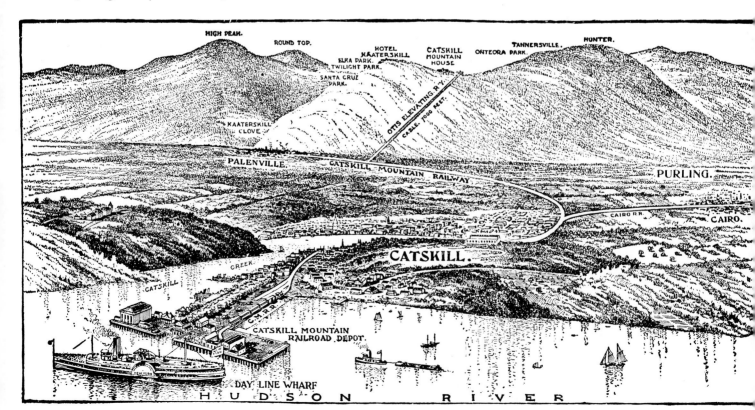

BIRD'S-EYE VIEW OF THE CATSKILLS FROM CATSKILL LANDING

CHAPTER TEN

On and Off the Rails

NDEED, when Secretary Charles Addison Beach submitted his financial statement for the Catskill Mountain Railway on June 30th, 1906, there was reason for optimism. He listed a surplus for each year since 1902, a surplus that had jumped from $1,528.48 in that year to $17,577.53 in the latest year. Interest on the first mortgage bonds had been paid and 5.83% was established as the rate for dividends on the first income bonds. Earnings were as follows:

Freight	$13,932.66
Shale freight	13,273.20
Passengers	47,498.27
Extra baggage	52.35
Express	497.10
Weighing and Confection machines	49.55
Gross earnings	$75,303.13

The favorable balance was achieved despite the expense of the new Otis connection ($5,744.94) and a new spur track to the stone dock ($219.33).[1] Not only was the little railroad providing a valuable service for the resort area and the steamboat lines, but it was actually turning a profit!

So, from April to November each year the diminutive trains whistled and rang their way from the landing to the mountains, claiming right-of-way over the twice-daily shale trains. Sleek and shining, Master Mechanic Driscoll's locomotives made a brave appearance, graceful American types with high drivers and tall smokestacks. Their painstaking reconditioning, each winter, employed the engineers full-time, assuring the railroad of reliable, almost pampered, steam motive power. In these years, engineer Frank Ruf earned the nickname of "The Flying Dutchman" because his coat tails whipped in the breeze as he guided the Cairo train on its two roundtrips daily. Jesse Oakley, distinguished by his disreputable derby and drooping mustache, piloted the engine on the Pa-

lenville accommodation. Charles L. Long shuttled his open shale cars between Cairo and Leeds and the brick kilns. And other personalities garnished the open platforms of the passenger cars — conductors Martin Brewer and Burr Vaughan posed resplendent in their brass-buttoned blue serge suits and uniform caps. To the young train-watchers, they were much to be admired.

Burgett Wolcott remembers asking one of the conductors who lived nearby if he could get work on the railroad. It was more than just a job he wanted, for, as he said, "There was lots of work on the farm, but I kind of wanted to go on the railroad." At about the same time, Sandy Phillips had a similar desire, and climbed the dark stairs of the Catskill Station to see Mr. Beach. Under interrogation, the young man revealed, "I'm 20." C. A. stroked his beard and shook his head. "Can't you be 21?" "Sure." "O. K. You're hired."

Both Wolcott and Phillips went a-railroading, one as trainman, the other as baggage master. Their days began at 5 a.m. when they started loading freight from the night boat, wrestling heavy barrels of ice-packed meat into the cars. Then their train service began. Wolcott made two round trips to Cairo (6:30 a.m. and 12 noon) and one to Palenville (at 3:30 p.m.) arriving at the Landing at 6:30 (unless Claude Heath was the substitute runner, when the time would be considerably better). Frequently, an extra late train was run, in which case the end of the day was near 10 p.m., a total of 17 hours of labor. Their pay was $40 a month.

Despite the long hours and strenuous tasks required of the slim-gauge railroaders, regardless of the rather treacherous right-of-way (the hairpin curve in Austin's Glen and the heavy grade on the Cairo line over George Duncan's property

CATSKILL MOUNTAIN RAILWAY

AND CAIRO RAILROAD

From Catskill Landing, on the Hudson River, to the Catskill Mountains, connecting at Otis Junction for the

OTIS ELEVATING RAILWAY AND THE CATSKILL & TANNERSVILLE RAILWAY.

CLOSE CONNECTIONS AT CATSKILL WITH HUDSON RIVER DAY LINE, CATSKILL NIGHT LINE AND NEWBURGH AND ALBANY LINE STEAMERS; ALSO THE NEW YORK CENTRAL AND WEST SHORE RAILROADS.

TIME-TABLE NO. 160.   TAKES EFFECT FRIDAY, MAY 20, 1910.

CONNECTING LINES — LEAVE NEW YORK / ARRIVE IN NEW YORK

READ DOWN

CONNECTING LINES	A M 9 00	A M 9 00	LEAVE ALBANY A M 8 30	LEAVE NEW YORK A M 8 30	P M *6 00	P M *6 00
Catskill Line Steamers						
H. R. Day Line Steamers, 42d Street	11 11	11 11	New York 7 54			
New York Central RR.	11 30	11 30	7 15	7 15		
West Shore RR. (42d Street)						

READ UP — ARRIVE IN NEW YORK

	A M *5 00	A M *5 00	P M 5 30	P M 5 30	P M 7 09	P M 7 09
Catskill Line Steamers						
H. R. Day Line Steamers	12 50	12 50	2 20	2 20	7 09	7 09
New York Central RR.	10 45	10 45	2 45	2 45	7 50	7 50
West Shore RR. (42d Street)						

Catskill to Cairo, Otis Summit and Palenville — READ DOWN

Friday, May 20, 1910.

STATIONS	DISTANCES	No. 1 Night Line Palenville & Otis R'y Special DAILY A M	No. 3 Night Line Cairo Special DAILY A M	No. 7 Otis R'y & Palenville Express DAILY EXCEPT SUNDAY A M	No. 9 Cairo Express DAILY EXCEPT SUNDAY NOON	No. 11 Day Line Otis R'y & Palenville Special DAILY EXCEPT SUNDAY P M	No. 13 Day Line Cairo Special DAILY EXCEPT SUNDAY P M
LEAVE Catskill Landing	.00	6 30	6 35	11 25	12 00	3 30	3 40
Catskill Village	.80	6 35	6 35	11 35	12 10	3 35	3 45
West Shore Station	1.25	6 40	6 40	11 40	12 15	3 38	3 50
3d Bridge Siding	4.10	8 6 28	8 6 28	11 48	12 23	3 46	3 58
Leeds (Toll Gate)	5.72	6 36	6 36	8 11 52	8 12 27	8 11 52	8 4 02
South Cairo	7.71	6 45	6 57	11 57	12 32	3 55	4 07
Cairo Junction	9.43	8 6 50	8 7 02	12 02	8 12 37	4 00	8 4 12
(Via Cairo Railroad) Arrive Cairo Leave	8.77		7 15		12 50		4 25
Lawrenceville	4.90			8 12 07		8 4 05	
M. H. Road	2.17			8 12 12		8 4 10	
Otis Junction	.67			12 16		4 14	
Palenville Arrive Leave	.00			12 24		4 22	
Otis Summit VIA OTIS RAILWAY, CONNECTING AT OTIS JUNCTION.		7 15		12 27		4 25	

Palenville, Otis Summit and Cairo to Catskill — READ UP

STATIONS	DISTANCES	No. 6 DAILY EXCEPT SUNDAY Cairo Day Line and Railroad Express A M	No. 8 DAILY EXCEPT SUNDAY Otis R'y Day Line & Railroad Express A M	No. 10 DAILY EXCEPT SUNDAY Cairo Afternoon Express P M	No. 12 DAILY EXCEPT SUNDAY Otis R'y Afternoon Express P M	No. 16 DAILY Cairo Night Line and Railroad Express P M	No. 18 DAILY Otis Night Line and Tannersville Night Line Special P M
Catskill Landing	15.75	10 35	10 50	2 45	3 00	6 15	6 30
Catskill Village	14.95	10 30	10 45	2 40	2 55	6 10	6 25
West Shore Station	14.50	10 25	10 41	2 35	2 51	6 05	6 21
3d Bridge Siding	11.65	8 10 16	10 33	8 2 26	2 43	5 56	6 13
Leeds (Toll Gate)	10.03	8 10 11	8 10 23	8 2 21	8 2 33	5 51	6 08
South Cairo	8.04	10 05	10 23	2 15	2 33	5 45	6 03
Cairo Junction	6.32	8 10 00	8 10 18	8 2 10	8 2 28	8 5 40	8 5 58
Cairo	3.77	9 50		2 00		5 30	
Lawrenceville			8 10 13		8 2 23		8 5 53
M. H. Road			8 10 08		8 2 18		8 5 48
Otis Junction			10 03		2 13		5 43
Palenville			9 53		2 03		5 33
Otis Summit		9 50		2 00		5 30	

Large figures indicate regular stops.

8 opposite small figure indicate that trains stop on signal or to let off passengers. *Catskill Evening Line Steamers do not leave New York on Sunday evenings or Catskill on Saturday evenings.

FOR THE INFORMATION AND GOVERNMENT OF EMPLOYEES ONLY.

THOS. E. JONES, General Passenger Agent, Catskill, N. Y.   CHAS. A. BEACH, Gen'l Supt., Catskill, N. Y.

OTIS SUMMIT is the Station for CATSKILL MOUNTAIN HOUSE and HOTEL KAATERSKILL.

The Otis Ry. connects at Otis Summit with the CATSKILL & TANNERSVILLE RY. for Laurel House, Haines Falls and Tannersville.

No. 2 in temporary repose. This early photo shows the typical glistening aspect of Catskill Mountain engines. (*Author's Collection*)

At the ferry slip. Just south of the steamboat dock and railroad station at the Landing, the streetcar waits for ferry passengers. (*A. Fred Saunders Collection*)

A formal portrait at the Landing. Back from the river's edge, engines 1 and 2 pause before beginning their day's duties, No. 2 on the shop lead and No. 1 in front of the engine house. *(Winfield W. Robinson Collection at Colgate University)*

being but two examples), notwithstanding the apparently haphazard method of train operation (the conductor and engineer of a train off its scheduled time simply telephoned the next station and made arrangements with the crew of an opposing train -- there was no dispatcher) and in spite of the confusion caused by the hectic transfer of passengers, baggage and freight from the boats to the trains, few accidents occurred.

The Otis funicular, or incline, as the locals called it, had great potentiality for disaster, it might seem. Yet the operation was managed so well that few incidents are known to have upset the regular, uneventful ascent and descent of the cars. Harry Jones recollects that one of the little Otis boxcars broke its coupling with the Otis train near the summit and rolled out of control down the mountain. But only a short distance from its

precipitous starting point, it lurched onto the safety switch and was shunted into the brush on the hillside, damaged but little. An "independent operator" on the Otis, one Hank Morton, worked in a hotel above and lived at home below. He took the early morning trip up, with his homemade "go-devil" parked in the baggage car behind. This box-like contraption was his vehicle for the down trip late at night, after the last Otis train had run. Basically a greased box with cleats beneath to hold it on the rails, the go-devil had a crude wooden friction brake. On one down trip, Hank misjudged his speed or lost the use of his brake and sailed off into the black night sky. He landed in a gully shaken, bruised and surrounded by splintered boards.[2]

The Otis towermen, whose life might seem uneventful (despite the ups and downs), sometimes

The Landing from above. From the upper deck of the steamboats, observers could sense the excitement as steaming trains and horse-drawn omnibuses waited for passengers. (*Steamship Historical Society of America, Inc., courtesy of Donald C. Ringwald*)

exhibited human failings that removed them from the purely functional category. Witness this letter, hand-written on Otis stationery:

Catskill, N. Y. July 3d 1908

Mr. T. E. Jones
   G. P. A.

The reason that the 11-20 run on Otis Ry. was not made on June 30th Will [William Driscoll, son of John and Otis engineer at the time] tells me is as follows — The men at the upper station got no signal from the Conductor at lower Station at 11.20

They waited 3 or 4 minutes and then went to Dinner — There [sic] dinner hour, or time, is between 11.20 and 11.50

I have written the Conductor to be more prompt in notifying Towerman about the running of cars.

Yours truly

Jno L. Driscoll[3]

Another towerman, out of pure cussedness, left Otis Conductor Elmer Mower and a companion stranded at the turnout halfway up the mountainside. Their trip was their home journey, since each ended the day at the wrong station. Walking the high trestles would have been a perilous undertaking, at best, so they decided to wait for assistance. The telephones provided on the cars now saved them from a cold and uncomfortable night on the chestnut seats. Another employee heard the persistent jingling of the towerman's phone bell and investigated. In a few minutes the men were safe, but there were other consequences. The towerman lost his job and a new man took his place. His first day on the job was more memorable than most, for he managed to place the up train in the middle of the engine room below him, amid splendid wreckage. He, too, was replaced.[4]

93

The Otis and the Mountain House. An Otis car crosses the last of several trestles before it arrives at the summit. *(Library of Congress)*

Below, starting up the Otis. Having loaded the baggage car, the crew prepares for the upward journey *(Author's Collecton)*

Other replacements became necessary when the engine shop burst into flames late in 1908. The most valuable piece of equipment lost was engine No. 4, leaving the company with no relief locomotive. Thus, second No. 4 came onto the roster, a locomotive identical in specifications but more modern in appearance than her predecessor. Second No. 4 was also named Charles L. Beach perpetuating the memory of the Grand Old Man of the Mountains, now gone to his rest. But the fire was not the only minor difficulty afflicting the Catskill Mountain Railway.

The year 1910, in particular, brought grief to the company. Appropriately enough, it was April first when Master Mechanic Driscoll wrote to Assistant Superintendent Jones that

> Mr. Finklestein in breaking up the old locomotive [probably first No. 4] used some dynamite.
>
> The charge was too close to our Pass cars. They broke 12 lights of Glass. I have seen him and he is to pay us 60¢ apiece for the Glass. Total $7.20.
>
> These glass cost us about 48¢. The difference will pay for Labor putting in Glass. He will be in to see you and you can settle the matter with him.[5]

Then, on April 2, the shale train was derailed near Leeds, spilling the new locomotive onto its side and remodeling the cab into an open-air job. Since the shale cars were owned by the brick company, they also shared the loss.

And Shale Brick soon found itself in real difficulties with its Catskill neighbors. On August 26, 1910, a subscription list was circulated among those residents most directly affected by the dense smoke rolling from the company's chimneys. The purpose of the subscribers was "to obtain injunctive relief restraining the operation of the plant in such manner as to interfere with the reasonable use and enjoyment of residential property in the village." Within a short time after the suit was instituted, the tall chimneys were built higher in order to pollute the air at a loftier level.[6] But Shale Brick had only a few years of life remaining, anyhow.

On the railroad line, on the next day, the train from Cairo jumped the track at the West Leeds schoolhouse. As Frank Ruf eased off slightly on the throttle for the slight curve, he felt the engine lift under him, pound along the ties and tip dangerously. In a moment, she overturned. The disconnected baggage car and coaches slid on by. The surprised occupants of the baggage car platform were two trackmen deadheading back from Cairo. For a terrible few seconds they became the front of the moving train of cars. Then the car imbedded itself in a trackside embankment, pin-

Otis Summit station and power house. A C. & T. accommodation has just backed off the wye to await the arrival of the incline car. Note the locomotive (probably an altered 1st No. 1) standing at the power house. *(Durham Center Museum)*

The remains of No. 4 after the blaze. The intense heat left only a locomotive skeleton; even the bell melted away. *(Durham Center Museum)*

Aftermath of the shop fire. On December 7, 1908, the C. M. Ry. lost its repair building as well as one-quarter of its motive power. *(Winfield W. Robinson Collection at Colgate University)*

The Shale Brick smoke nuisance. This photo by William Reynolds supported the complaint of home-owners near the brick kilns. (*Reynolds Collection at the Greene County Historical Society, deposited by Mrs. Livingston Cody*)

The Shale Brick plant. In an attempt to mollify its neighbors, the company raised its chimneys, having completed one here and starting on a second. The C. M. Ry. caboose is barely visible on the left track. (*Author's Collection*)

The wreck scene. With the tender and baggage car out of the way, the railroad crew concentrated on the locomotive and passenger car. (*A. Fred Saunders Collection*)

Below, the coach on a firm footing. Upright again, the first coach is prepared for re-railing. (*Iva Cammer Collection*)

No. 2 as a photographer's prop. Before repair crews arrived, summer visitors found the overturned locomotive to be a photogenic perch. *(Alan Ruf Collection)*

ning them by the legs. When the jacks relieved the pressure, the men were found to be sound, although frightened by the experience.[7]

Even though no passenger was hurt, at least one traveler took no chances, as this letter in the company files indicates:

> Mr. T. C. Jones
>   Catskill, N. Y.
> Dear Sir: —
>   Will you please return the money on this ticket. I got it the day of the wreck at Leeds and one of our party was afraid to come by train.
>   Truly yours
>   Bertha Apkes
>   Palenville
>   Greene Co.
>   N. Y.

Other mishaps did occur, but the pile-up at the stone schoolhouse was the most sensational in the history of the narrow gauge lines. And even here, personal injury and equipment damage were light.[8] Probably because of the infrequency of regular trains and the rarity of extras, there were no head-on collisions (excepting one gentle nudge when a passenger train bumped a construction train in Austin's Glen during the first years of operation). The most frequent accident was derailment, often where schoolboys were likely to congregate. Never proved, the suspicion persisted that small hands with bricks (shale, of course) caused most of these "accidents."

More important to management than these annoying incidents were plans for the future. Even the appearance of the automobile on Greene County's dusty roads did not pose any serious threat to the life of the system (a Kissel Kar began a passenger run from Catskill to Cairo in 1911).[9] The transportation revenue shared by the Catskill lines with their railroad rival, the Ulster & Delaware, remained substantial.

When the directors of the Catskill Mountain Railway Company met on December 5th, 1911, optimism seemed the dominant mood. President Beach received authorization to purchase a new steam locomotive to replace the ailing CHARLES T. VAN SANTVOORD, No. 3. The builder selected to fill the order was the Rogers Company of Paterson, New Jersey, the same firm reputed to have worked on the Canajoharie & Catskill's MOUNTAINEER. And, oddly enough, extension of the C. M. Ry. along the ancient C. & C. route became a topic for serious discussion at this same gathering. It was even proposed that widening the gauge in order to accept standard railroad cars be investigated, at least between Catskill and Cairo.[10]

To those with a long memory, the plans must have seemed familiar.

99

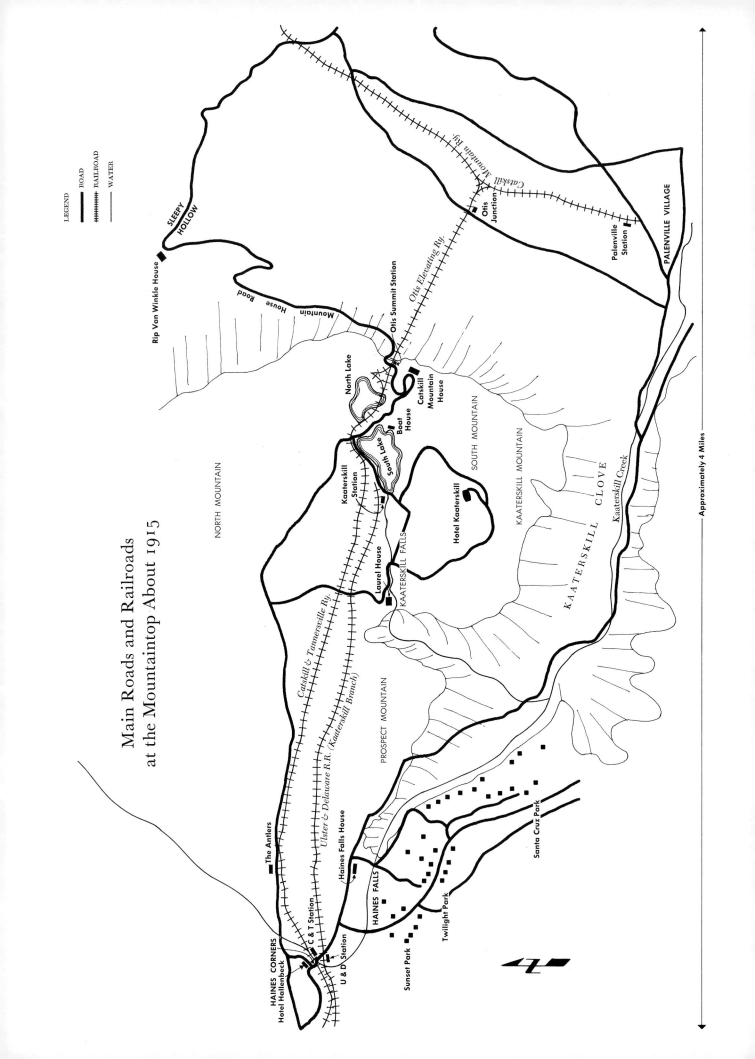

Main Roads and Railroads
at the Mountaintop About 1915

LEGEND

ROAD
RAILROAD
WATER

SLEEPY HOLLOW

Rip Van Winkle House

Mountain House Road

Otis Elevating Ry.

Otis Summit Station

Otis Junction

Catskill Mountain Ry.

Palenville Station

PALENVILLE VILLAGE

North Lake

Boat House

Catskill Mountain House

South Lake

SOUTH MOUNTAIN

KAATERSKILL MOUNTAIN

Kaaterskill Station

KAATERSKILL FALLS

Laurel House

Hotel Kaaterskill

KAATERSKILL CLOVE

Kaaterskill Creek

NORTH MOUNTAIN

Catskill & Tannersville Ry.

Ulster & Delaware R.R. (Kaaterskill Branch)

The Antlers

PROSPECT MOUNTAIN

Haines Falls House

HAINES FALLS

Twilight Park

Sunset Park

Santa Cruz Park

C & T Station

U & D Station

HAINES CORNERS

Hotel Hallenbeck

Approximately 4 Miles

CHAPTER ELEVEN

The Run Downhill

THE enthusiastic optimism that led Catskill Mountain Railway directors to order a new locomotive and to contemplate expansion of their system was echoed in other quarters. The Catskill & New York Steamboat Company accepted from Marvel shipyards a new steel-hulled passenger steamer in 1911, the *Clermont*, to replace the elderly *Kaaterskill*. For freight, the American Car & Foundry Company delivered to them a new propeller-driven freighter, the *Storm King*, to take over for the smaller *W. C. Redfield*.[1] The financial investment embodied in these two river boats testified to a firm belief that the New York-Catskill Mountains transportation lines had a prosperous future.

Sharing in this belief were the proprietors of the Catskill Mountain House, Charles (not Charles *Addison*) and George H. Beach, as well as their fellow hosts in the hotels and boarding houses. As if to reassert the social prestige that formerly attached to the "pioneer of the Catskills" (as their advertisements put it), the hotel was made the scene of a notable social event.

On June 29, 1911, at seven in the evening, a special train departed from Catskill filled with well-dressed and distinguished guests, some from as far away as Puerto Rico. Besides the unusual appearance of the passengers, ladies and gentlemen in formal evening attire, the very fact of a special train movement on the narrow gauge drew attention. Even freight extras were uncommon on the line. The locomotive gleamed from polishing and the coaches looked immaculate for the journey down Water Street, along the Glen and into the twilight shadow of the peaks. At Otis Junction the train swung into the station and unloaded the bridal party and guests for the wedding of Mary Lindsey Beach, daughter of George H. Beach, the son of C. L. Beach and co-manager of the Catskill Mountain House, to John K. Van Wagonen.

The powerful searchlight on the Ledge directed its beam on the Otis car so that it could be seen from miles away. Then, when the leisurely climb was over, the party entered a Mountain House lavishly decorated with mountain laurel, fern fronds and wild pink roses. The bridesmaids carried shepherd's crooks festooned with pink carnations, with which they formed an arch for the bride and her father as they approached the Reverend Doctor C. G. Hazard, the officiating minister, and performed this duty again as the bride and groom left the drawing room platform. Dancing followed, with Professor Brundage's orchestra playing appropriate selections. Soon supper was served and the guests prepared to leave.

At 11:30, the reception ended and the Otis transported the bridal party down the incline, illuminated as before by the blinding shaft of light from the searchlight. All in all, the affair had been the high point of the season in the Catskills.[2]

Among those attending had been representatives of the old resort families, most notably the Schutts of the Laurel House and the Hardings of the Kaaterskill Hotel. Their hostelries were considered the best in the area and continued to enjoy excellent reputations.

The Laurel House was an outgrowth of Peter Schutt's boarding house, built in 1846. The rapid expansion and immediate popularity of the Laurel House came from its remarkable natural setting, as did the success of the Catskill Mountain House. The latter possessed an unparalleled vista of the Hudson and distant mountains; the former had Kaaterskill Falls. Waters from Spruce Creek and the two lakes combined on Schutt's farm and dashed over a precipice for 180 feet to another

The Mountain House about 1915. The old hotel became the site for conventions, meetings and reunions in later years and somehow less genteel. The searchlight may be seen just at the left of the flagpole. *(Mrs. C. A. W. Beach)*

Twilight Rest Club-House. In addition to the resort hotels and boarding houses, cottage colonies with social centers dotted the slopes near Haines Corners and Tannersville. *(Library of Congress)*

The Laurel House. Not far from the "Huckleberry" line flowed the Kaaterskill Falls in the front yard of the Laurel House. *(Library of Congress)*

Palenville Hotel. At the foot of the difficult road up the Kaaterskill Clove stood this popular stopping-place for man and beast. Both horse and driver filled up before the journey. *(Library of Congress)*

Below, the Antlers Hotel. Proprietors Butler and Leggett claimed this to be the "largest and most select House at Haines Falls." It rated a platform stop on the C. & T. Railway. *(Library of Congress)*

The Haines Falls House. Modest hotels also lined the Kaaterskill Clove, this one furnishing access (for its 80 guests) to the cascade known as Haines Falls. *(Library of Congress)*

Below, the transportation center, Haines Corners. Both the U. & D. (background) and C. & T. depots can be seen in this view taken from an upper story of the Hollenbeck Hotel (later the Renner House). *(Library of Congress)*

Haines Corners Station. When the railroad and No. 2 were new, crew and passengers stood for this photographic gem. *(Library of Congress)*

Returning home via C. & T. The accommodation for the Otis, Catskill Mountain and steamboat lines, below, loads passengers at Haines Corners. *(Robert Harding Collection)*

The "Huckleberry" train. From left to right, Brakeman Arthur Dowling (on rear steps), Brakeman Herbert O'Hara (in baggage compartment door), conductor Percy Gardner, unidentified passenger, fireman Wesley Lewis and engineer Edward Warner. *(Winfield W. Robinson Collection at Colgate University)*

ledge, then plunged another 80 feet into the gorge. An enterprising man, Mr. Schutt built steps to the lower levels for his hotel patrons and for other paying customers. Because the water supply varied in volume, he built a dam above the drop so that he could, in effect, turn the falls on or off at will.

The Hotel Kaaterskill achieved its fame at a later date than the others, but the fact that it was constructed on a grand scale gave it an architectural integrity and unity of plan not characteristic of either of the older resorts. Its 1890 capacity was 1,500 guests; the limit for the Mountain House was 400. The three hotels controlled a vast recreational area filled with natural wonders.

Other lodging houses had sprung up on the mountains, of course. R. Lionel De Lisser noted, for example, that "Tannersville is one vast boarding-house."[3] And some vacationers had joined park associations, by which members could occupy cottages and share in activities at central club-houses. In this way, Twilight, Elka, Sunset and Santa Cruz parks came into being alongside the resort hotels. Smaller or less view-oriented houses were able to fill their rooms almost every season. The Catskills-bound traveler had a multitude of choices for his stay.

Along "Resort Ridge," from Otis Summit to Tannersville, the Huckleberry rolled along its serpentine route parallel to the Ulster & Delaware's standard gauge line. The secondhand locomotives first placed in service soon wore out and brand new Baldwin moguls replaced them (in 1901 and 1908). These engines, unlike those of the Catskill Mountain Railway, had outside frames which partly masked the driving wheels. In appearance they were squatty and ungainly machines lacking the graceful proportions of the C. M. Ry. American types. However, they were more than

A C. & T. depot shed. One of several small structures serving the mountain-top hotels, this is probably Laurel House platform (*Author's Collection*)

Near Laurel House Station I. In 1910, photographer Edward B. Johnson caught No. 1 as she rounded one of the many sharp curves on the route. (*Winfield W. Robinson Collection at Colgate University*)

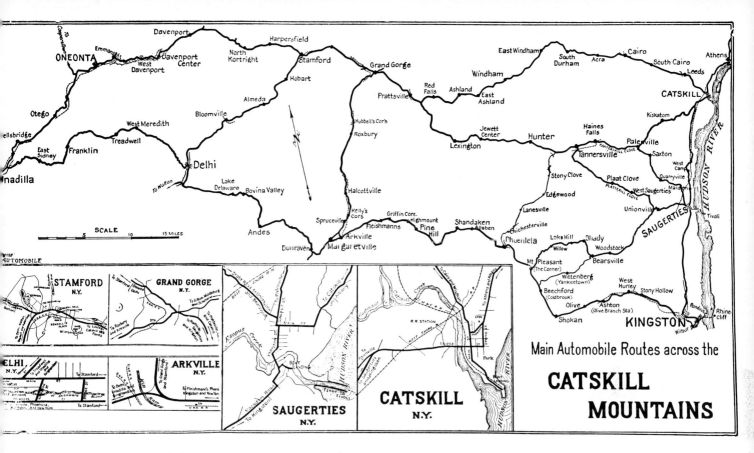

Automobile map of the Catskills. Van Loan's 1909 *Catskill Mountain Guide* included this motorist's aid, in a handbook which had formerly shown only railroad routes.

adequate to handle the light trains and to keep their footing on the rudely-laid track.

Eight trains each way daily shuttled up and down the line, with an extra late train on Saturday. The wooden coach and combine creaked to a stop not only at the regular agency stations — Otis Summit, Haines Corners and Tannersville — but at sheds and platforms at Laurel House, Sunset View, the Antlers and Clum Road. Speed was slow for the five miles, understandably, averaging twelve miles per hour for the run. Although berry-picking stops were not sanctioned by the company, a one minute pause for sightseeing was. The sight to see was Kaaterskill Falls, a clear view of which could be had from the car windows. Regularly the timetable listed "Kaaterskill Falls" — neither a station nor a flag stop — just magnificent scenery. At Tannersville was the only turntable on the road; a wye served to reverse the train at Otis Summit. Incoming trains ran first onto one leg of the wye and back out on the other until the last car touched the bumper at the Otis connection. At the end of the wye, alongside

North Lake, the company had erected a winter storage shed for C. & T. equipment.

Construction and reconstruction were constant on all three lines, as the railroads' reports to the Public Service Commission for 1912 demonstrate. Despite losses for the C. & T. of $2,582, for the Otis of $5,104 and for the Catskill Mountain of $3,497, management replaced the old Corliss boilers at the Otis power station with two new Sterling vertical boilers of 150 horsepower each, and it repaired and repainted the C. M.'s Palenville station.[4] Although losses continued in the 1913 statements (totaling about $4,500), the Catskill Mountain company retained a bridge engineer to examine and adjust bridge trusses. They also installed a wye at Palenville and pulled out its timeworn turntable. For this year, the PSC inspector could find only one fault with any of them — and this was on the basis of appearance, not operation or maintenance. He found offensive the penciled names, messages and other *graffiti* covering the walls of the Cairo passenger station and considered distasteful the vulgar poster displays on its

freight depot. Obviously, here was an inspector with artistic sensibilities.

"Vulgar displays" of another kind were occurring with increasing frequency in the ruggedly romantic Austin's Glen, between 1912 and 1917. Silent movie makers from eastern studios satisfied themselves that the hills, woods and rocky glades just west of Catskill village were far enough west for western movies. On one of these films, *The Badmen*, actors and cameramen were regularly interrupted by the passing of Catskill Mountain trains. For them, the narrow gauge was a nuisance and of little interest to film makers.[5]

Of interest and concern to the railroad, however, was the shutdown of the shale brick plant in 1912. Dependent upon a fluctuating demand, Tidewater Paving Brick either boomed or closed in direct response to orders or the lack thereof. Not until October of 1912 were the shale trains running, with Conductor Utter in his accustomed place — the boxcar-caboose behind the open clay and shale cars.[6] The regular trains delivering raw materials ran for almost two years more, when the shale brick plant closed down for good. Its last sizable order was for 10,000 special brick for the Ashokan Dam and then the buildings were

closed.[7] The loss to the railroad was considerable, for in good years the shale trains earned half of the company's freight income and one-fifth of its total receipts.

The railroads had also been deprived of another valuable asset when Charles Addison Beach died suddenly of apoplexy in 1913. This capable manager of the little system had overseen the everyday functioning and the major reconstructing of all three lines in the mini-system. In conjunction with John Leonard Driscoll, he had performed his duties well. It is fortunate, perhaps, that he did not live to see the destruction of his work.

A brief news item in the *Catskill Recorder* in June of 1914 will serve to illustrate the revolution in transportation that would doom the little trains:

> 900 barrels of asphalt for contractors Rice and Leone arrived in Catskill by boat and were sent to Acra via the Catskill Mountain R. R. The asphalt will be used on the new state road there.

The automobile age had arrived and, with it, the demand for better highways. Within a few years, the motor car would become the national mania so that even the high country of the Catskills would be not merely visited but invaded. News accounts

Cairo depot. Although teams of horses still outnumber the jitneys, the automobile age had come to the Catskills. *(Durham Center Museum)*

witness to the tenacity of the duster-clad, goggled motorists:

> Some touring cars come up the [Kaaterskill] Clove road, but the occupants say that generally, the last part of the way, they have to be towed.

And again:

> The roads were oiled again recently, so several automobiles skidded into the ditch.[9]

Although the Hudson River Day Line had cheerfully subsidized the Catskill railroads, viewing this cost as necessary to their own profitable operation, in the year 1915 the Olcott family had second thoughts. The Catskill Evening Line, in which they had invested heavily, was consistently losing money; Catskill was losing its popularity as a landing place for passengers. The narrow gauge lines reported a total net loss of over $12,000. Consequently, between May and August of 1915, the three railways went into bankruptcy and receivers were appointed.[10]

It was apparently the intention of the Day Line to lop off the railroad passenger service as soon as possible by eliminating all but freight traffic on the Catskill & New York Steamboat line and by ripping up the railroad track to be sold as scrap. But opposition from hotel interests, Catskill citizens and, ultimately, the State Public Serv-

ice Commission, resulted in continued operation. During 1915, the company juggled its tariff schedules, generally raising freight rates and lowering passenger fares, but the deficit persisted.

On April 25, 1916, the railroad properties were sold to a corporation consisting of Eben E. Olcott and Alfred Van Santvoord Olcott of the Day Line, George H. Beach and John K. Van Wagonen of the Catskill Mountain House, Edwin H. Snyder of the Catskill & New York Steamboat Company and three Catskill men, William Palmatier, H. C. Wilbur and John L. Fray.[11] An attempt by Catskill banker James P. Philip to purchase the lines failed when he did not meet the court's deadline for consummation of the deal. Mr. Philip mistrusted the intentions of the new corporation and insisted that a continuation of the same management would result in disaster for the railroads and for the community.[12]

Whether Philip could have saved the system from its eventual fate is doubtful. The three companies (including the leased Cairo Railroad) became one corporation under the title "The Catskill Mountain Railroad," still firmly under the control of the Day Line. Stockholders[13] in the new venture were as follows:

111

No. 2 upset. In a picture reminiscent of those of big-game hunters posing with their kill, these boys stand by the monster they probably bagged with a shale brick. (*Winfield W. Robinson Collection at Colgate University*)

A trio of engines at the Point. Numbers 1, 2 and 5 drowse in the railroad yard before they are called on for another day's work — if that day ever comes. (*Author's Collection*)

Beach family	110
Hudson River Day Line and Olcott family	697
Catskill Evening Line	21
Thomas E. Jones	1
Howard C. Wilbur	1
John L. Fray	1
William Palmatier	1
Total	832

In the local railroad office, Thomas E. Jones carried out the duties recently performed by Charles A. Beach and tried to keep the trains running.

In April and May of 1918 the *Examiner* and the *Recorder* reported track repairs under way on the Otis, Catskill & Tannersville and Catskill Mountain segments of the new system. Economies were effected in other ways, however. Train service was drastically curtailed — to three trains each way where ten or twelve had been customary in peak years. Anticipating the final outcome, two trusted Otis employees did not return for the summer season. William Driscoll, engineer (and son of John L.) and James Halcott, towerman, declined contracts for the summer season.[14]

The employees who did remain found some excitement, however. On June 29, the train from the west jumped the track at Greene Street and the engine overturned. Engineer William Coffin recalls that several dozen eggs he was carrying in the tender of Number 2 escaped unharmed, as did he and his fireman, Ed Loveland. He also believes that the derailment could be blamed on the small boys who plagued trainmen with their dangerous antics at the crossing. On the eastbound trip he had opened the steamcocks to "discourage" them from standing so close to the track. Among the six passengers on the five coaches was Super-

intendent Jones, who supervised the repair work. The road was soon back in operation.[15]

Its days were numbered, however. An undated "Statement made by the Catskill Mountain Railroad Corporation," probably used at a PSC hearing and now in the company's files at the Bronck House, lists four reasons for abandoning the entire system. First, the company could not get competent men to operate the railroad safely and those available demanded large increases in wages. Secondly, there was a difficulty in obtaining coal and supplies, as well as a higher cost. Third, the increased competition of autos (which had already caused discontinuance of Cairo passenger service) had reduced revenues significantly. Fourth, the United States Railroad Administration takeover had resulted in rates unfavorable to the company. The deficit for 1917 was $5,536.06; the estimate of loss for 1918 was $12,000 or more. If operation could be maintained, the statement continued, the Day Line would share the loss up to $2500 for the season.

No one appeared to assume the remainder of the annual loss.

Clearly, the time of its usefulness was over. During April and May of 1919, the light patina of rust on the narrow gauge rails turned a deeper brown, for no vacationer-laden coaches would burnish them again. The engine whistles chiming in the Glen, as regular each spring as the chirping of the first robin, would be heard no more. For the first time in thirty-six years the Catskill newspapers carried no notice of the first train of the season.

The season for the little red trains had already ended.

113

The second bridge disaster. Dismantling this abandoned bridge resulted in death for two men. It remained as they left it for many years. *(Winfield W. Robinson Collection at Colgate University)*

CATSKILL MOUNTAIN RAILROAD

EFFECTIVE MAY 7, 1917.

An abbreviated timetable.

CATSKILL TO CAIRO						CAIRO TO CATSKILL					
		NO. 3	**NO. 9**	**NO. 13**				**NO. 6**	**NO. 10**	**NO. 16**	
STATIONS	DISTANCES	DAILY EXCEPT SUNDAY	DAILY EXCEPT SUNDAY	DAILY EXCEPT SUNDAY		**STATIONS**	DISTANCES	DAILY EXCEPT SUNDAY	DAILY EXCEPT SUNDAY	DAILY EXCEPT SUNDAY	
		Morning Local	Freight and Express	Railroad Express				Railroad Express	Afternoon Freight and Express	Evening Local	
		A M	NOON	P M				A M	P M	P M	
Catskill Landing...Lv	.00	7 00	12 00	3 30		Cairo.................Lv	.00	9 50	2 00	5 45	
Catskill Village.........	.80	7 05	12 10	3 35		Cairo Junction.........	3.77	s 10 00	s 2 10	s 5 55	
West Shore Station...	1.25	7 10	12 15	3 40		South Cairo..............	5.49	10 05	2 15	6 00	
3rd Bridge Siding......	4.10	7 18	12 23	3 48		Leeds (Toll Gate).....	7.48	s 10 11	s 2 21	s 6 06	
Leeds (Toll Gate).....	5.72	s 7 22	s 12 27	s 3 52		3rd Bridge Siding......	9.10	10 16	2 26	6 11	
South Cairo..............	7.71	7 27	12 32	3 57		West Shore Station..	11.95	10 25	2 35	6 20	
Cairo Junction..........	9.43	s 7 32	s 12 37	s 4 02		Catskill Village.........	12.40	10 30	2 40	6 25	
Cairo ....Ar	13.20	7 45	12 50	4 15		Catskill Landing...Ar	13.20	10 35	2 45	6 30	
		A M	P M	P M				A M	P M	P M	

Large figures indicate regular stops.   Trains do not run Sundays

s Opposite small figures indicates that trains stop on signal or to let off passengers.

Passenger and Freight Service to Lawrenceville, M. H. Road, Otis Junction, Palenville, Otis Summit, Laurel House Station, Antlers, Haines Falls and Tannersville will be resumed May 18, 1917.

CHAPTER TWELVE
Echoes in the Glen: An Epilogue

THE sad task of winding up the railroad's business fell to Thomas E. Jones. Preparing a list of railroad properties and equipment, an inventory that included a velocipede (for use by track inspectors and workers) and a boarding house (for railroad workers at Otis Summit), Jones received authorization from Supreme Court Justice Charles E. Nichols to conduct a private sale on August 16, 1919. The rails and fixtures were sold to M. K. Frank of Pittsburgh, whose crews began to salvage the rails at Palenville. Frank Ruf, a veteran of thirty years in engine service, fired up a locomotive for the final rites:

> The saddest job I ever had over those years was to run the engine that hauled a train of flat cars when the road closed down and they were taking up the rails. As we moved down nearer and nearer to Catskill I looked back over the roadbed and could not believe that I would never again run an engine over it.[1]

The end had come, but the story was not over. Scraps and pieces of the once-busy little railroads remained to be disposed of. Though the roadbed from Catskill Landing to Cairo, to Palenville and to Tannersville now lay bare, the yard trackage near the steamboat wharf was left in to hold the idle equipment.

The two best locomotives, Catskill & Tannersville's Nos. 1 & 2, were shipped to New Jersey to be nearer prospective buyers, in late 1919. These undoubtedly were loaded on Ulster & Delaware tracks adjacent to the C. & T. and arrived at the Hoisting Machinery yards in late October and early November of 1919. There they would sit for almost five years. The Catskill Mountain's youngest locomotives, No. 4 and No. 5, were sold by the Railway Equipment Company to a Georgia lumber railroad. Numbers 1 and 2 did not find buyers; they were still on company property at the Landing in 1926 and were, presumably, scrapped.[2]

The cars found a readier market. The two Huckleberry coaches and combination car were converted to metre gauge by the Townley firm and shipped south in September of 1919. All of the Catskill Mountain passenger cars and three of the four baggage cars found a new home with the National Railways of Mexico in early 1920. The other freight cars, with four exceptions, were off company property within the next three years.[3]

In February of 1922, a crew accepted a subcontract from the Kingston Scrap & Iron Co., their work to be the dismantling of the second railroad bridge, near the Van Vechten homestead. On the twenty-third day of the month, as the five workmen were loosening bolts, the entire western span gave way, crushing out two lives between the girders and the creek ice. Two others were injured and the job was abandoned.[4] Reminiscent of the Canajoharie & Catskill bridge disaster, the unexplained accident at the second bridge seemed to suggest that the railroad was not ready to die. For many years, until scrap prices rose sharply in the pre-World War II period, the bridge remained, its fallen segment rusting away in the Catskill stream.

During the 1920s and 1930s the automobile took over the tasks formerly performed by the Catskill railroads. Though the narrow gauge system ceased operation at an early age, the rival Ulster & Delaware trackage to Kaaterskill and Hunter remained in for another twenty years. Until February 21, 1940, occasional trains visited the mountain tops, although passenger business had evaporated and freight traffic was light. Removal of the onetime Stony Clove & Catskill Mountain-Kaaterskill railroads effectively isolated the Cats-

Main Street tunnel. Excavation of the cut to the Landing also undercut Main Street, so a tunnel was constructed. *(Author's Collection)*

Through the completed tunnel, at right, can be seen the other overhead bridges made necessary by the railroad's deep furrow. The side track leads to Shale Brick. *(A. Fred Saunders Collection)*

kill heights once again, just as they had been in 1830, before the Canajoharie & Catskill travesty. But the very fact of the survival of the U. & D.'s branch from Phoenicia so long after the demise of its slender-sized competitor calls for explanation.

As a short-haul, passenger-carrying, non-standard-width railroad network, the Catskill Mountain-Otis-C. & T. route could not effectively meet the rivalry of the motorcar. It had no direct link with other railroads; its only interchange was with the steamboats at Catskill Landing. When passenger traffic patterns altered, when autos gave vacationers flexibility of time and route, when river steamers appeared by comparison too slow and old-fashioned, when all-rail routes promised speed and convenience, the three-sectioned narrow gauge system spiked down to the Catskill waterfront could neither adapt nor adjust. On the other hand, the Ulster & Delaware (now officially the Catskill Mountain Branch of the New York Central) could not only offer through rail service for passengers from the metropolis but could depend upon long-haul freight business into the area. The narrow gauge's small territory could be covered adequately by motor trucks and jitneys.

The year that saw the end of railroad service to Hunter and Kaaterskill brought a blazing reminder of the Catskill Mountain Railroad. On a cold February evening in 1940 the last remaining railroad structure at Catskill caught fire and created orange-yellow patterns on the village waterfront. The engine house-shop was reduced to a skeleton of charred wood.[5] The fire removed, once and for all, the railroad from the old steamboat landing.

Lost in the next year was another enduring vestige of the Catskill narrow gauge lines. John Leonard Driscoll died on January 2, 1941, at the great age of 103. Before his death he achieved the distinction of being the oldest railroad man in the country, his life beginning in the earliest days of railroading (during the short and calamitous career of the Canajoharie & Catskill), spanning the growth period (when he became involved in the vain narrow gauge experiment) and ending at the dawn of the Diesel age.[6] More than any other person, J. L. Driscoll had been identified with the railroads. In a real sense, it was his railroad and, at his passing, the Catskill Mountain lines faded a little farther into the past.

Today only the patient, curious visitor to the northern Catskills can discover traces of the railroads. The roadbed, remarkably, is still discernible near the main highways. Even the Canajoharie & Catskill embankments and cuts can be seen between Cairo and Cooksburg if the investigator is willing to hike through the underbrush some distance from the automobile routes. Converted railroad buildings, like those at Otis Junction, are visible here and there. Bridge abutments and piers still stand, the first bridge still in use, in fact, for water and gas mains. But, though the physical evidence remains, memories of the life of the railroads are scarce and dimming fast.

Times have changed and the Catskills have changed with them. The great hotels have vanished from the peaks, the night boats no longer steam along the river and the diligent little engines scuttle into the foothills no more. Having fulfilled their mission, the little railroads withdrew from the wooded heights and the bouldered valleys.

The steam engine's invasion of the Catskills had been rebuffed. The haunts of Rip Van Winkle — the misty tarns, the stony crags, the shadowy forests, the slender waterfalls and the precipitous mountain cloves — would revert to wilderness again.

No more whistles echo in the glen.

The *Onteora* as an excursion boat. In 1922 the *Onteora,* minus her staterooms, became a commuter between the metropolis and Bear Mountain. *(Steamship Historical Society of America, Inc.)*

The first bridge — then. A very early photo (note the headlamp) of No. 1 as she begins her run on a sunny Catskill morning.
(Edward Vogel Collection)

The first bridge — now. The village of Catskill still finds use for the old railroad span — as a pedestrian bridge, for gas and for water lines. *(Photo by the author)*

Notes

In general, sources are provided here in abbreviated form; complete source identification can be found in the bibliography which follows. However, individual items from the manuscript collections are cited fully.

CHAPTER ONE — Rip's Realm

1. Thoreau, p. 361.
2. For a thorough history of the Mountain House, its origin, popularity, decline and destruction, see the recent book by Roland Van Zandt.
3. Gordon, p. 471.
4. Bishop, p. 681.
5. Gordon, p. 472.
6. Abt, pp. 59, 65.
7. Meyer, p. 285; *Senate Document No. 180.*
8. *Assembly Document No. 232.*
9. *Biographical Directory; Who Was Who.*

CHAPTER TWO — Tom Cooke & Co., Railroad Builders

1. Pickell, pp. 5-17. The lieutenant later invested in five shares of the railroad's stock.
2. *Ibid.*
3. McNeill, pp. 6-20.
4. *Ibid.,* pp. 21-23.
5. Ephraim Beach, *Remarks,* p. 10.
6. Vedder, *History,* p. 81.
7. *Circular,* p. 1. Although Albany's commercial interests might have felt Catskill to be a potential rival if the railroad succeeded, there is no evidence for an "Albany Conspiracy" against it. Stock subscription lists published in *Senate Document No. 106* show no Albany residents who held stock and refused to pay their assessments.
8. Hammond, pp. 450-451.
9. Beach *v.* Cooke, p. 107.
10. Nelson Smith, letter to Hiram Smith, April 14, 1832. From the Van Vechten papers, courtesy of Mrs. Van Vechten and M. P. Smith.
11. Sands Higinbotham, letter to John J. DeGraff, March 15, 1831. Jervis papers.
12. J. L. Stagg, letter to Alexander Thompson, Sept. 24, 1831. Thomson papers.
13. *Catskill Recorder,* May 23, 1839.
14. Ephraim Beach, manuscript.
15. *Beach Family Magazine,* p. 84.
16. Beach *v.* Cooke, p. 49.
17. *Catskill Association,* p. 1.
18. Circular, [p. 1].
19. Gerstner, *Die innern communicationen,* p. 235.
20. Brodhead, p. 28.
21. *Railroad Iron Imported,* p. 2; *Senate Document No. 59.*

CHAPTER THREE — Out on the Line

1. Ephraim Beach, manuscript.
2. *Senate Document No. 59.*
3. Vedder, "Greene County — Railroads" pp. 3-4. Mrs. Mabel Parker Smith has brought to my attention a long epic poem entitled "Catskill," which appeared in installments in the *Catskill Messenger* in April, 1837. One section describes the effects of the railroad and of purchase by the Land Association upon the VanVechten Homestead, birthplace of Abraham VanVechten, "father of the New York Bar." Interesting as the poem is to the historian, a longer selection than this would be tedious. These few lines are tedious enough:

   > These ornamented grounds lie desolate;
   > These stately trees that waved o'er beauteous
   >   slopes,
   > By fellers' hands now strewed in fragments lie;
   > The trees that bent with fruits from Eden Sprung
   > Are plucked by passers' hands, and none rebuke;
   > These halls are desolate from silence thrilling —
   > That dwelling fair, its very cornerstone
   > Which time had failed to lessen,
   > Now must yield to the improvers power;
   > The beauteous knoll is marred to fill yon hollow;
   > And in the room of gentle solitude
   > Wooing to thought and fastening our hearts
   > By interlacing tendrils to the throne
   > Of God, our portion, here shall sound the roar
   > Of railroad train thundering down the gorge,
   > All level, straight, and stiff, and stereotyped,
   > When nature poured her beauty's store
   >   abundant . . .

4. N. Y. *Laws,* Ch. 321 (1837).
5. *Assembly Document No. 165* (1838).
6. *Senate Document No. 106* (1839), p. 85.
7. Letter, Ephraim Beach to George H. Cooke [sic], June 4, 1838. Cook papers. For this information I am indebted to Jean W. Sidar, who is preparing a biography of George Cook.
8. Cook, memoir.
9. *Ibid.*
10. *Ibid.*
11. *Ibid.*
12. *Senate Document No. 106.*
13. *Ibid.*
14. Letter to Cook from Lewis Germain, Feb. 4, 1839.
15. March 28, 1839.
16. Letter, July 1, 1839.
17. May 3, 1839.

CHAPTER FOUR – Smoke on the Horizon

1. Cook, memoir.
2. L. J. Germain, letter to George H. Cook, January 13, 1839.
3. Letter, February 19, 1839.
4. Unfortunately no source is given for this information. The account also notes that the company shipped the engine *twice* to New Jersey for repairs before its use was abandoned. Not only was it not returned to the manufacturer, a logical move, but it was sent to a shop at Paterson having no rail connection, necessitating a trip overland by horse power, according to Beers. Because Beers is patently wrong about the locomotive's failure, this additional information can be doubted, too. Perhaps this is an example of how local "history" grows – by gross exaggeration and faulty association. It was well-known that the Rogers Locomotive Works of Paterson, New Jersey, had no railroad connection. This odd fact may have remained in some local antiquarian's memory along with recollections of the Canajoharie & Catskill's difficulties.
5. Gerstner cites the presence of the engine at the time of his visit in 1839, but notes no problems; White, p. 112.
6. Walton Van Loan recalled that Hank Hibler was the teamster. *Catskill Recorder*, May 6, 1910.
7. J. B. Bassinger, letter to Cook, Dec. 16, 1839.
8. Ephraim Beach ms. As of Oct. 1, 1839, the actual construction cost, according to Beach, was $283,-266.35, but the company paid only $248,262.39. The new contract was in two sections, one to the 22nd mile, the other to the 26th.
9. John Baldwin, reported in Vedder, *History of Greene County, N. Y. 1800-1830*, undated typescript.
10. Arbitration Bond, in the Durham Center Museum.
11. Ephraim Beach ms.; Howland, p. 250; *Catskill Messenger*, May 7, 1840. Beers gives the wreck date as March 4, an error that has been repeated in later works.
12. Ephraim Beach ms.
13. *Ibid.* An inherent flaw in Town lattice bridges was noted by H. Haupt, *American Railroad Journal*, Oct. 1, 1840. He found them too frail for heavy loads and in need of additional braces or arches. The C. & C.'s unfortunate experience was not an isolated one.
14. *Circular*, p. 3. The Cooksburg depot was undoubtedly constructed by Orrin Phelps, who received $120.00 in June, 1841 as part payment. Chadwick, p. 59. Mather in his geological survey of the Catskills notes the appearance of limestone "along the railroad" and shale "at the Depot on the railroad near Potter's Hollow." Both he and Beck made inspection trips along the right-of-way but, good scientists that they were, they made no more than casual references to the Canajoharie & Catskill and then only as a reference point.
15. Brodhead, p. 29.
16. *Catskill Messenger*, May 14, 1840.
17. Chadwick, pp. 58-61.
18. Peter Mesick, letter to Mr. Thompson, April 9, 1841. Thomson papers.
19. *American Railroad Journal*, Oct. 15, 1840.
20. Brodhead, pp. 32-33.
21. Poor, p. 251.

CHAPTER FIVE – The Trackless Pathway

1. Jenkins, pp. 451-452.
2. This account is a compilation from the Hudson & Berkshire documents cited in the bibliography.
3. Hudson & Berkshire documents; Salsbury, pp. 171-172.
4. Hough, p. 324.
5. Beach *v.* Cooke contains testimony about financial disagreements between the two men, not only pertaining to this land suit but to other arrangements.
6. The full story of the Day Line appears in the recent book by Donald C. Ringwald. (See Bibliography.) Beach *v.* Cooke reveals that both Alfred Van Santvoord and his father Abraham had at least a tenuous connection with the Canajoharie & Catskill through a modest investment in the Catskill Land Association.
7. Van Loan, *1890*, p. 89; Bruce, p. 66.
8. Fleming's volume gives a good introductory account of narrow gauge railways in this country.
9. Vail, pp. 490-492. C. L. Beach, despite his surname, was not related to Ephraim Beach. Ephraim's descendants left Catskill either just before or shortly after his death in 1857.

CHAPTER SIX – Rip's Depot

1. *Examiner*, Sept. 11, 1880.
2. *Ibid.*, Sept. 25 and Oct. 2, 1880.
3. Charles L. Beach ms.
4. Executive Committee Record Book.
5. Dec. 4, 1880.
6. *Examiner*, Jan. 1 and Jan. 8, 1881.
7. *Ibid.*, Jan. 8, 1881.
8. Ringwald, pp. 142-143. Ringwald's book is an interesting account of the Day Line, with some occasional references to the Catskill-New York company. Adequate histories of the Catskill and other less glamorous lines remain to be written.
9. *Examiner*, Feb. 12, 1881.
10. *Ibid.*, Feb. 26, 1881.
11. *Ibid.*, Nov. 12, 1881.
12. Saunders, vol. I, p. 75.
13. *Ibid.* The Kaaterskill had two bridal chambers among its 121 staterooms, and according to the New York *Maritime Reporter* of July 22, 1882, she would "equal, if not excel, any night boat on the Hudson River."
14. *Ibid.*, p. 96.
15. *Examiner*, Jan. 28, 1882.
16. *Ibid.*
17. *Ibid.*, Mar. 18, 1882. According to the May 20th *Examiner*, John B. Halcott designed a standard station building of two stories, 25' x 16', with 50' platforms, to be built at Palenville, South Cairo and Mountain House Station. Only the Palenville structure conformed to the pattern.

18. *Catskill Daily Mail*, February 3, 1941; *Examiner*, April 22, 1882.
19. *Examiner*, April 29 and May 27, 1882. The first two locomotives were named for directors who were solid supporters and bondholding boosters of the railroad — S. Sherwood Day and John T. Mann. Mann had been the C. & C.'s receiver and S. Sherwood Day had promoted the unsuccessful Catskill & Schenectady. The *John T. Mann* arrived on June 3.
20. Vedder, "Railroads," p. 7; *Examiner*, July 29 and August 5, 1882.
21. Saunders, I, p. 85; *Examiner*, August 5, 1882.
22. *Examiner*, August 12, 1882.
23. *Ibid.*, September 2, 1882.
24. Lillie, p. 527.
25. *Examiner*, December 2, 1882.

CHAPTER SEVEN — A Slide for Titans

1. *Examiner*, November 10, 1883.
2. *Report of the Board of Railroad Commissioners*, II, 1884, pp. 194-196.
3. *Examiner*, May 9, 1885.
4. *Ibid.*, June 6, 1885.
5. *Report*, I, 1892, p.
6. *Examiner*, June 27 and July 11, 1885.
7. Work must have been inconvenient for these men, since no shop or engine house was provided until 1890. In the absence of positive information, it may be speculated that previously repairs were made while engines were in the shelter of the covered platform at the Landing, which also had two closed-in waiting rooms, one at each side of the tracks.
8. *Recorder*, January 15, 22, 29, 1885.
9. The certificate of incorporation was filed on September 14, 1892, shortly after completion of the Otis.
10. Memoranda in Catskill Mountain Railroad papers.
11. *Recorder*, July 15, 1892; Otis Catalog.
12. *Ibid.*; Report, II, 1893, p. 324.
13. *Albany Argus*, June 1, 1892; *Recorder*, July 1, 1892. Judge Walter Bliss allowed me to inspect the survey map of the Cooperstown line in his possession. Other schemes for the area were rampant. The April 29th *Recorder* carried a notice of the organizational meeting of the *Davenport, Middleburgh & Durham*. As late as 1894, the S. C. & E. D. was amending its charter so as to locate from Cairo rather than from South Cairo.
14. *Recorder*, Dec. 1, 1892.
15. *Examiner*, June 10, 24, 1893; *Recorder*, June 2, 1893.
16. *Examiner*, July 22, 1893.
17. *Report*, II, 1893, pp. 266-268.
18. July 15, 1892.

CHAPTER EIGHT — Gains and Losses

1. Newland, 1914, pp. 23-31.
2. *Recorder*, Dec. 14, 1894.
3. *Ibid.*, July 2, 1897.

4. *Ibid.*, Nov. 27, 1896.
5. *Report*, II, 1898, p. 147.
6. From May 11 to September 1, 1896, the railway received 2,445 fares from West Shore station, about 8% of the total passengers carried. *Recorder*, Sept. 18, 1896.
7. Railroad inspectors for the Kaaterskill and Stony Clove & Catskill Mountain railroads noted consistently the sturdiness and width of bridges, suggesting that the management would eventually widen the gauge if the route proved valuable to the Ulster & Delaware.
8. *Report*, I, 1899, pp. 335-336. Company correspondence mentions a gasoline motor car, plans and photos of which were submitted to the Directors for consideration.
9. Timothy Dwight, that untiring traveler, "found whortle-berries in abundance and perfection" in this same locality in 1815.
10. *Report*, II, 1900, p. 449.
11. Ringwald, p. 92.
12. Charles Beach ms.

CHAPTER NINE — Good Years

1. All figures (rounded out to the nearest 1,000) are taken from the *Railroad Commissioners' Reports* for the appropriate years.
2. Saunders, II, pp. 81-87. Commissioned in 1898, the *Onteora* was 236 feet long, 35 feet in the beam and was believed to be capable of 20 m. p. h.
3. *Reports*, II, 1905, p. 262.
4. *Ibid.*; C. M. R. R. Sale List. After dissolution, the Otis cars were advertised as of 8-ton capacity. This may reflect the weight limitations for incline use (5-tons) as opposed to possible capacity (8-tons) on a level roadbed, rather than an exaggerated claim for selling purposes.
5. Reported in the *Stamford Mirror*, May 4, 1939.
6. Letter to the author, August 18, 1966.
7. *Reports*, I, 1905, p. 33.
8. *Rules and Regulations of the Catskill Mountain Railway*, Revision of May 1, 1906.
9. *Reports*, II, 1899, p. 138; II, 1905, p. 135.
10. Company correspondence for March alludes to the fire and, incidentally reveals the "dual-lives" lived by some of the employees. A copy of a letter to Martin Brewer of New York City, who toured with a minstrel show each winter, assured him that his summer job as conductor on the C. M. Ry. was waiting for him.

CHAPTER TEN — On and Off the Rails

1. The statement is in the Yale University Library.
2. Phillips, Jones and Coffin remember the Morton car; obviously, no blueprints are available.
3. This letter is in the railroad's correspondence file at the Bronck House.
4. These stories of the Otis were supplied by Harry Jones.
5. Letter in the railroad's correspondence file.

6. The original list is in the Reynolds Collection (presented by Mrs. Livingston Cody) at the Bronck House. Mrs. M. P. Smith supplied me with a photocopy.

Among the complainants are two individuals who wished to remain anonymous. But opposite "Citizen No. 2," has been written "Ruf." Perhaps this was Engineer Ruf of the C. M. Ry., whose desire for anonymity would be understandable.

7. *Recorder*, Sept. 2, 1910; Wolcott. Burgett Wolcott recalls that two physicians from Catskill were called but were not needed, "medicinal" whiskey having been administered by a good samaritan from one of the nearby boarding houses. Miss Iva Cammer remembers that the spectators were mostly boarders from the Maple Rest, just across the road from the scene.

8. B. Wolcott supplies two other wreck stories. In one derailment near Leeds, he was standing in the baggage car door and was thrown *through* a fence. Untouched by the barbed wire, he was nevertheless so shaken that he took a week off to recover. Another time the locomotive and tender stayed on the rails, but the first car hit the ties. On this last train of the day only the crew and a newly-wed Cairo couple were riding. At least a part of their wedding night was spent in the cab of No. 2, where they stood with other crew members on the return to Catskill, leaving the rest of the train behind.

9. The Catskill trolley line began service at the turn of the century between the Landing and Leeds, but it was never as popular with patrons as the railroad, for it did not extend far enough to compete for summer traffic. Its shaky financial record and short chronological history testify to its ineffectiveness as a rival.

10. *Recorder*, December 8, 1911.

CHAPTER ELEVEN — The Run Downhill

1. Saunders, I, pp. 98-102.
2. Details of the occasion are from the *Catskill Daily Mail*, June 29, 1911 and the *Catskill Recorder*, June 30, 1911. A statement in the correspondence files headed "Present Holding — C. M. Ry. Co. 1st Income Bonds" notes that "stock remains the same with the exception of $1,000.00 which George H. Beach has transferred to John K. Van Wagonen." Van Wagonen became sole proprietor of the Mountain House in 1930.
3. *Picturesque Catskills*, p. 66.

4. *Reports of the Public Service Commission, 2nd District*, II.
5. *Albany Times-Union*, September 29, 1957. A short, rather amateurish film of the railroad was shot during this period. Prints are still available from Blackhawk Films.
6. *Recorder*, October 11 and 25, 1912.
7. *Ibid.*, August 7, 1914. Sporadic attempts were made to reopen the plant and operate it successfully, but the business could not be revived. The high labor cost of laying individual bricks in pavement could not be tolerated and concrete and macadam pouring of street and road surfaces became common.
8. *Ibid.*, August 3, 1917.
9. *Ibid.*, August 17, 1917, from the Haines Falls news.
10. *PSC Reports*, 1916.
11. *Ibid.*
12. *Examiner*, April 29, 1916; flyer headed "To: Bond owners and stockholders" in the railroad's files.
13. From a stockholder's list dated January 30, 1919.
14. *Recorder*, April 6, 1918.
15. *Ibid.*, July 5, 1918.

CHAPTER TWELVE — Echoes in the Glen

1. Saunders notes. The engine was probably #5, the newest on the roster. Ruf's assigned locomotive, #2, had been damaged in the June 1918 derailment and, according to the sale list, was still unrepaired.
2. Information is from letters and statements of account in the company's correspondence files. On February 15, 1926, the Hoisting Machinery Company advised against sending #1 and #2 to New York, citing a handling charge of $3500 as a minimum. This would have been much more than the intrinsic worth of the engines.
3. Insurance policies among the C. M. R. R. papers show that locomotives #1 and #2, the caboose and three flat cars were the only equipment insured by Jones in 1922.
4. *Recorder*, February 24, 1922; *Daily Mail*, February 23 and 24, 1922.
5. *Daily Mail*, February 2, 1940. At one time the railroad had spaces for four engines — the original single engine house with an attached open-sided shed for two locomotives and a two-stall enclosure for storage and repairs.
6. *Railway Age*, January 14, 1941, pp. 190-191.

A last reminder of the Catskill Mountain Railway. In 1940, the old engine house at the Landing caught fire, destroying the last structure at the once-busy yard. (*Alan Ruf Collection*)

Bibliography

Manuscripts, Papers and Other Collections

Beach, Charles L. Typewritten manuscript outlining the life and achievements of C. L. Beach. In the possession of Mr. and Mrs. Charles A. W. Beach, Catskill, New York.

Beach, Ephraim. "Canajoharie & Catskill Rail Road and matters connected therewith." Holograph citing Beach's grievances against the company. In Vedder Memorial Library, Bronck House, East Coxsackie, New York.

Catskill Mountain Railroad. Miscellaneous papers. Scattered correspondence from the early years becoming more complete files for the bankruptcy and receivership years. Contains minutes of the meetings of the executive committee of the Catskill & Tannersville, minute book of the Otis Railway, secretary's book for the South Cairo & East Durham Company and payroll information for the later years. In the Vedder Memorial Library.

Catskill Shale Brick Company. "Article of agreement . . . November, 1894 between the Catskill Mountain Railway and the Catskill Shale Brick Company . . ." In possession of Mrs. Francis P. Rivette, Mycenae, New York.

Cook, George Hammell. Papers, including correspondence 1838-1840 about Canajoharie & Catskill matters and an account of his own employment by Ephraim Beach. In the Rutgers University Library.

Hill, M. Harry. "A Lost Day in the Catskills." Typescript by a C. M. Ry. employee. In the possession of Howard Muller, Catskill.

Jervis, John B. Papers. Some references to the Canajoharie & Catskill, like the Sands Higinbotham note on the railroad's prospects and a letter of application from C. R. Alton who served as rodman under Captain Beach on the 1831 survey. In the Jervis Library, Rome, New York.

Powers, James. Papers. Records of land speculation, business and legal correspondence and miscellaneous materials. No direct references to the C. & C. R. R. which Powers seems to have favored but not to have supported financially. An interesting collection mirroring Catskill affairs in the 19th century. In the New York State Library, Albany, New York.

Robinson, Winfield W. Albums of railroad materials. Pictures, timetables and letters concerning various short lines and abandoned routes. As a State Police officer, Captain Robinson traveled widely in the state and collected wherever he traveled. In the Colgate University Library.

Saunders, A. Fred. Two albums of steamboat and railroad items. Mainly Hudson River maritime material, but including some items on Catskill railroads. In the Catskill Public Library, Catskill, New York.

Saunders, A. Fred. Rough notes on Catskill's railroads. Consists largely of information on former employees. In Vedder Memorial Library.

Smith, Nelson. Letter to Hiram Smith of Leeds, New York, dated April 14, 1832. In the William Van Vechten home, Leeds, New York.

Thomson Collection. Papers of the family's mercantile association in Catskill. The correspondence of J. A. Thomson, 1802-1844, contains references to C. & C. stock, the departure of J. B. Bassinger and a cryptic, angry note from Daniel Akerley, apparently dissolving their partnership in the ferry business. In the New York State Library.

Vedder, Jessie V. V. "Railroads of Greene County." Unpublished typescript. In Vedder Memorial Library.

Books and Printed Materials

Abt, Henry Edward. *Ithaca*. Ithaca, New York: Ross W. Kellogg, 1926.

Adams, Charles Francis, Jr. *Notes on Railroad Accidents*. New York: G. P. Putnam's Sons, 1879.

Barber, John W. and Henry Howe. *Historical Collections of the State of New York*. New York: S. Tuttle, 1842.

Beach, Ephraim. *Remarks, accompanied by a Letter of Report of Capt. E. Beach, Engineer, on the Feasibility of a Railroad Intersecting the Canajoharie & Catskill Railroad, and Extending along the Valley of the Susquehannah, and from thence to Lake Erie; With the Opinion of Benjamin Wright, Esq., Civil Engineer, Confirming the Practicality of the Undertaking*. New York: J. M. Danforth, 1831.

Beach v. Cooke. Catskill: Joseph Joesbury, 1863.

Beach Family Magazine, I (January 1, 1926).

Beck, Lewis C. *Mineralogy of New York*. Albany: W. & A. White and J. Visscher, 1842.

Beers, F. W. *Atlas of Greene County, New York*. New York: F. W. Beers, A. D. Ellis & G. G. Soule, 1867.

Biographical Directory of the American Congress, 1774-1961. Washington: United States Government Printing Office, 1961.

Bishop, J. Leander, A. M., M. D. *A History of American Manufactures from 1608 to 1860*. Third Edition. 3 vols. Philadelphia: Edward Young & Co., 1868.

Bradford, T. G. *An Illustrated Atlas, Geographical, Statistical and Historical of the United States and Adjacent Countries.* Boston: Weeks, Jordan & Co., 1838.

Brodhead, Edward H. *Report of the SURVEYS AND ESTIMATES of a Route for the Proposed CANAJOHARIE AND CATSKILL RAIL-ROAD from Cookesburgh to Canajoharie, and of the Examination of that which is Constructed, Made under the Directions of William C. Bouck, Peter Osterhout, Sr. and Ezra Hawley, Esqrs., Committee.* Catskill: William Bryan, 1842.

Bruce, Wallace. *The Hudson River by Daylight: New York to Albany.* New York: John Featherston, 1874.

Buckman, David Lear. *Old Steamboat Days on the Hudson River.* New York: The Grafton Press, 1907.

Burr, David H. *Map of the State of New York.* 1834.

Carmer, Carl. *The Hudson.* New York: Farrar & Rinehart, 1939.

Carter, Charles Frederick. *When Railroads Were New.* New York: H. Holt, 1909.

Catskill Association, formed for the Purpose of Improving the Town of Catskill, in the County of Greene, State of New York, and for other Purposes. December 28, 1836. New York: Mitchell & Turner, 1837.

Chadwick, George Halcott and Mrs. Jessie Van Vechten Vedder. *The "Old Times" Corner (1929-1930).* Catskill, New York: Greene County Historical Society, 1932.

Chapin, William. *Squire's Map of the State of New York.* 1834.

Charter, Officers and Directors of the Catskill Mountain Railroad Company. September, 1880. Catskill, New York: M. A. Trowbridge, 1890.

Chevalier, Michel. *Histoire et Description des Voies de Communication aux États-Unis et des Travaux d'Art Qui en Dépendent.* 2 vols. Paris: Librairie de Charles Gosselin, 1840.

Circular. "The Undersigned, Directors of the Canajoharie and Catskill Rail Road Company, deem it proper to lay before the Stockholders the following sketch of the history of this Company . . ." Dated Feb. 10, 1841.

Coman, K. *The Industrial History of the United States.* New York, 1910.

DeLisser, R. Lionel. *Picturesque Catskills.* Northampton, Mass., 1894. [Reprinted by Hope Farm Press, Cornwallville, N. Y., 1967]

Durrenberger, Joseph Austin. *Turnpikes.* Valdosta, Georgia: Southern Stationery and Printing Co., 1931.

Dwight, Timothy. *Travels in New-England and New-York.* 4 vols. London: William Baynes and Sons, and Ogle, Duncan & Co. and H. S. Baynes and Co.: Edinburgh, 1823.

Earle, Alice Morse. *Stage Coach and Tavern Days.* New York: Macmillan, 1901.

[Ellis, Franklin] *History of Columbia County, New York.* Philadelphia: Everts & Ensign, 1878.

Fleming, Howard. *Narrow Gauge Railways in America.* Second edition. Lancaster, Pennsylvania: Inquirer P. & P. Co., 1876.

Flick, Alexander C., editor. *History of the State of New York.* 10 vols. New York: Columbia University Press, 1934.

French, J. H. *Gazetteer of the State of New York.* Sixth edition. Syracuse: R. Pearsall Smith, 1860.

Gallt, F. A. *Dear Old Greene County.* Catskill, New York, 1915.

Gerstner, Francis Anthony Chevalier de. "Finances of the State of New York," *Journal of the Franklin Institute* (October, 1840), 223-227.

Gerstner, Franz Anton, ritter von. *Die innern communicationen der Veringten Staaten von Nordamerica.* 2 vols. Wien: L. Forster's artistische austault, 1842-1843.

Gillespie, W. M. *A Manual of the Principles and Practice of Road-Making.* New York: A. S. Barnes & Co., 1850.

Gordon, Thomas F. *Gazetteer of the State of New York.* Philadelphia: T. K. and P. G. Collins, 1836.

Halsey, Francis Whiting. *The Old New York Frontier.* Port Washington, Long Island, New York: Ira J. Friedman, Inc., 1961.

Hammond, Jabez D. *The History of the Political Parties in the State of New-York.* 2 vols. Albany, New York: C. Van Benthuysen, 1842.

Haney, Lewis Henry. *A Congressional History of Railways in the United States to 1850.* Bulletin of the University of Wisconsin No. 211. Madison, Wisconsin, April, 1908.

Haring, H. A. *Our Catskill Mountains.* New York: G. P. Putnam's Sons, 1931.

Haskins, Vernon. "The Canajoharie-Catskill R. R.," *Schoharie County Historical Review* (Spring, Summer, 1965), 29-30.

Hill, Henry. *Recollections of an Octogenarian.* Boston: D. Lothrop and Company, 1884.

History of Greene County. New York: J. B. Beers, 1884.

Hodge, P. R. *The Steam Engine, its Origin and Gradual Improvement.* 2 vols. New York: D. Appleton & Co., 1840-41.

Hough, Franklin B. *Gazetteer of the State of New York.* Albany: Boyd, 1873.

Howland, S. A. *Steamboat Disasters and Railroad Accidents in the United States. To which is Appended Accounts of Recent Shipwrecks, Fires at Sea, Thrilling Incidents, &c. (Vignettes.)* Worcester: Dorr, Howland & Co., 1840.

Hudson and Berkshire Rail Road. Letter from the Secretary of War. Jan. 21, 1829. Doc. No. 89, House of Representatives, War Department, 20th Congress, 2d session.

Hudson and Berkshire Rail-Road Report, Containing the Charter of Said Incorporation, Surveys, Estimates, &c. made at a meeting of the Citizens of Hudson, April, 1835.

Jenkins, John S. *History of the Political Parties in the State of New-York.* Auburn, New York: Alden & Markham, 1846.

Kindig, R. H., E. J. Haley and M. C. Poor. *Pictorial Supplement to Denver South Park & Pacific.* Denver: Rocky Mountain Railroad Club, 1959.

A Letter to the President of the Town of Catskill. January 10, 1838. New York: G. Mitchell, 1838.

Lillie, Lucy C. "The Catskills," *Harper's New Monthly Magazine*, LXVII (September 1883).

Lincoln, C. Z. *Messages of the Governors of New York.* Albany, 1909.

Longstreth, T. Morris. *The Catskills.* New York: The Century Co., 1918.

Mack, Arthur C. "C. and C. Railroad Begins Operations with Fanfare, Glance at History Shows," *Examiner-Recorder,* November 16, 1950.

Mack, Arthur C. "Greene County's Own Pioneer Railroad," *Examiner-Recorder,* October 26 and November 2, 1950.

Mack, Arthur C. "Greene County's Pioneer Railroad," *Examiner-Recorder,* October 19, 1950.

Mack, Arthur C. "Press Paid Little Heed to Early Rail Project," *Examiner-Recorder,* Nov. 23, 1950.

Mack, Arthur C. " 'Rejoicing in Catskill' Over a New Rail Project," *Examiner-Recorder,* Nov. 9, 1950.

Mack, Arthur C. "Reminder of the Past," *Railroad Magazine,* XLVII (February 1949), 88-95.

Mack, Arthur C. "Tragedy at High Rock Ends Career of C. of [sic] C. Railroad, Writer Reports," *Examiner-Recorder,* Dec. 14, 1950.

Mack, Arthur C. "When the Trains Ran Through Catskill," *Examiner-Recorder,* July 19, 1956 and July 12, 1956.

McNeill, William Gibbs. *Report on the Surveys of a Route for the Proposed Canajoharie and Catskill Rail-Road.* New York: Sleight and Robinson, 1831.

Mann v. Pentz. Catskill: Joseph Joesbury, 1849.

Mather, J. H. and L. P. Brockett. *A Geographical History of the State of New York.* Utica: John W. Fuller & Co., 1853.

Mather, William W. *Geology of New York, Part I.* Albany: Carroll & Cook, 1843.

Meyer, Balthasar Henry. *History of Transportation in the United States before 1860.* Washington: Carnegie Institution of Washington, 1917.

Morse's North American Atlas. New York: Harper & Brothers, 1842.

New York: A Guide to the Empire State. Compiled by workers of the Winters' Program of the Works Project Administration in the State of New York. New York: Oxford University Press, 1940.

New York State Assembly Documents.

New York State Senate Documents.

The New York State Tourist. New York: A. T. Goodrich, 1840.

Newland, D. H. *The Mining and Quarry Industry of New York State.* New York State Museum Bulletin 174. Albany, 1914.

Oliver, Smith Hempstone. *The First Quarter-Century of Steam Locomotives in North America.* Washington, D. C.: Smithsonian Institution, 1956.

Otis Catalog, 1913.

Phelps' Travelers' Guide Through the United States. New York: Horace Thayer & Co., 1853.

Pickell, Lieut. John. *Report of the Examinations and Surveys of a Route for a Rail-Road from Canajoharie, situated on the Erie Canal, to the Village of Catskill on the Hudson River.* Catskill: Faxon & Elliott, 1831.

Pierce, Harry H. *Railroads of New York, A Study of Government Aid, 1826-1875.* Cambridge, Massachusetts: Harvard University Press, 1953.

Pinckney, James D. *Reminiscences of Catskill.* Catskill: J. B. Hall, 1868.

Poor, Henry Varnum. *History of the Railroads and Canals of the United States.* New York: J. H. Schultz & Co., 1860.

Railroad Iron Imported: Letter from the Secretary of the Treasury. Doc. No. 18, House of Representatives, 26th Congress, 1st Session.

Ratsch, Carl. "Marker Erected by Historians," *Examiner-Recorder,* Oct. 19, 1950.

Reports of the Board of Railroad Commissioners. Albany, 1883-1906.

Report of the Directors of the Hudson and Berkshire Rail-Road Company. With the Engineer's Report to the Board. Hudson: P. Dean Carrique, Printer, 1837.

Reports of the Public Service Commission. 2d District. 1907-1920. Albany, 1908-1921.

Ringwald, Donald C. *Hudson River Day Line.* Berkeley: Howell-North, 1965.

Robinson, Captain Winfield W. "The Catskill Mountain Lines," *Railway & Locomotive Historical Society Bulletin No. 37* (May, 1935), 7-14.

Salsbury, Stephen. *The State, the Investor, and the Railroad: The Boston & Albany, 1825-1867.* Cambridge: Harvard University Press, 1967.

Sinclair, Angus. *Development of the Locomotive Engine.* New York: A. Sinclair, 1907.

Smith, J. Calvin. *Map of the State of New York.* New York: J. Disturnell, 1842.

Smith, Mabel Parker. *Greene County, New York: A Short History.* Catskill, New York, 1963.

Sowers, D. C. *Financial History of New York State.* New York, 1914.

Stevens, Frank Walker. *The Beginnings of the New York Central Railroad.* New York: G. P. Putnam's Sons, 1926.

Stuart, Charles B. *Lives and Works of Civil and Military Engineers of America.* New York: D. Van Nostrand, 1871.

Sweet, Frederick A. *The Hudson River School and the Early American Landscape Tradition.* New York: Whitney Museum of American Art, 1945.

Swift, William Henry. *Report of the Survey of the Route of the Ithaca and Owego Rail-Road.* Ithaca: Mack & Andrus, 1828.

Tanner, H. L. *New Universal Atlas.* Philadelphia: Carey & Hart, 1845. [N. Y. S. map copyrighted 1840]

Tanner, H. S. *A Description of the Canals and Rail Roads of the United States comprehending Notices of all the Works of Internal Improvement Throughout the Several States.* New York: T. R. Tanner & J. Disturnell, 1840.

Tanner, H. S. *The Travellers' Hand Book for the State of New York, The Province of Canada, and Parts of the Adjoining States.* Third edition. New York: The Geographical Establishment, 1845.

Thoreau, Henry D. *The Journal of Henry D. Thoreau,* ed. Bradford Torrey and Francis H. Allen. Vol. I. Boston: Houghton Mifflin, 1949.

Town, Ithiel. *Some Account and Description of Ithiel Town's Improvement in the Construction and Practical Execution of Bridges, Ducts and Rail-Roads.*

Vail, R. P. H. "Along the Hudson in Stage-Coach Days," *The Outlook,* LXXX (Saturday, June 24, 1905), 489-496.

Vandewater, Robert J. *The Tourist, or Pocket Manual for Travellers on the Hudson River, The Western Canal, and Stage Road, to Niagara Falls.* Second ed. New York: Ludwig and Tolefree, 1831.

Vandewater, Robert J. *The Tourist, or Pocket Manual for Travellers on the Hudson River, the Western and Northern Canals and Railroads: The Stage Routes to Niagara Falls; and Down Lake Ontario and the St. Lawrence to Montreal and Quebec. Comprising also the Routes to Lebanon, and Interesting Details.* Sixth ed. New York: Harper & Brothers, 1838.

[Walton Van Loan] *Van Loan's Catskill Mountain Guide.* New York: Rogers and Sherwood, 1890. New York: The Dudley Press, 1909.

Van Zandt, Roland. *The Catskill Mountain House.* New Brunswick: Rutgers University Press, 1966.

Vedder, Jessie V. V., compiler. *Official History of Greene County, New York.* Published by authority Greene County Board of Supervisors, 1927.

White, John, Jr. *American Locomotives: An Engineering History, 1830-1880.* Baltimore: Johns Hopkins, 1968.

Who Was Who in America. Historical Volume. 1607-1896. Chicago: A. N. Marquis Co., 1963.

Periodicals

American Railroad Journal
Catskill Daily Mail
Catskill Examiner
Catskill Examiner-Recorder
Catskill Messenger
Catskill Recorder
Greene County Examiner-Recorder

Former Employees Consulted

Banks, Perry. Mr. Banks assisted his father, Allen, in the engineering of the Otis Elevating Railway. He was later employed by the Hudson River Day Line as Chief Engineer of the *Washington Irving.* His home is in Catskill.

Coffin, William P. Mr. Coffin fired in 1913 and 1914 on the shale train and was put on as engineer of the Cairo train in 1915. Still hale and hearty in late 1968, he was living in his trailer home with his wife on Spook Hollow Road, Catskill.

Jones, Harry E. The son of Thomas E. Jones, Mr. Jones served as clerk and auditor in the railroad office in 1915 and 1916 before he entered the U. S. Army in 1917. In his 76th year, Mr. Jones retains vivid memories of the narrow gauge which he has generously shared. His home is near Kiskatom.

Phillips, Alexander ("Sandy"). As a young man Mr. Phillips was employed as baggage master (between 1911 and 1917). He now lives in Catskill.

Wolcott, J. Burgett. Mr. Wolcott worked as rear trainman in 1910 and then as Adams Express messenger until about 1914. He and his brother live in the century-old brick house at Leeds built by Jeremiah Burgett, having stopped active farming only recently. He is now 82.

The tarnished "Jewel of the Catskills." Before the State of New York burned it to the ground, the Mountain House stood, an empty, neglected relic of the past. *(Photo by Milton Wagenfohr)*

The Catskill Mountain House as it was. This meticulously constructed model of the old hostelry is the only tangible representation of the venerable Mountain House. It is displayed at the Bronck House. *(Photo by Milton Wagenfohr)*

The route of the incline. Bogart Road no longer over-passes the Otis but the dilapidated bridge still does, minus its floor timbers. Although more than fifty years have passed the old roadbed is still distinct from here to the summit. *(Photo by the author)*

Piers for the second bridge. The second bridge has gone, but the masonry supports still stand, useless monuments to the narrow gauge. *(Photo by Edward Bond)*

127

Above, No. 1 in later years. After extensive changes in John Driscoll's shop, the DAY sports a steel cab, straight stack, streamlined domes, new headlight and relief letters and numbers on the cab. (Author's Collection)

At left is No. 2, the JOHN T. MANN. Poor as it is in detail, this picture of the MANN posing at a wayside crossing is the earliest one available. It shows one difference from the 1883 shot of No. 1; the diamond smokestack may have been replaced as was No. 1's.
(William Bissinger Collection)

At left is No. 2 after overhaul. Master Mechanic John Driscoll stands beside a "streamlined" No. 2, with modifications accomplished in the company shops. (William Gordon Collection)

Below No. 3 poses for a formal portrait. This photograph is one of many that Frank Ruf took (who appears here at left) as reminders of his railroad service. Note that the tender is lettered "C. R. R." for the Cairo Railroad. (Alan Ruf Collection)

Appendix A

LOCOMOTIVE ROSTERS

The information supplied in the following lists is self-explanatory, for the most part, but the column headed "Specifications" requires some interpretation. The first figure in the column is the diameter of the driving wheels, the second and third the cylinder diameter and length of stroke, and the fourth the total weight of the locomotive. These specifications are the latest from company records and may not be the same as those when built. The last column contains brief facts on the operation and final disposition of each engine.

In all cases, the material presented here has been carefully checked against the best contemporary and modern authorities. These sources are cited at the end of each roster.

Few records exist to describe positively the Canajoharie & Catskill locomotive and to identify accurately the used Colorado & Southern engines acquired by the Catskill and Tannersville. Any uncertainties are indicated in appended notes.

CANAJOHARIE & CATSKILL

No.	Name	Type	Builder & No.	Date	Specifi-cations	Service & Disposition
—	Mountaineer	4-2-0*	H. R. Dunham & Company	1838-9	56	Said to have been dismantled and boiler used at ice-house at the Point.

*Brown lists this engine as a 4-4-0, but Dunham is believed to have built only the 4-2-0 wheel arrangement, so the 4-4-0 designation is probably an error. See also page 31.

Sources: Brown, Catskill Messenger, Catskill Recorder, Fisher, Gerstner, White.

CATSKILL MOUNTAIN (AND CAIRO)

No.	Name	Type	Builder & No.	Date	Specifi-cations	Service & Disposition
1	S. Sherwood Day	4-4-0	Dickson #335	1882	48 13x18 50,000	On final roster. At Landing until 1926.
2	John T. Mann	4-4-0	Dickson #336	1882	48 13x18 50,000	On final roster. At Landing until 1926.
3	Charles T. Van Santvoord	4-4-0	Dickson #522	1885	48 13x18 51,000	Delivered as No. 1 of Cairo R. R., then No. 3. Out of service 1911. Cannibalized and scrapped.
4	Charles L. Beach	4-4-0	Schenectady #4333	1895	49 13x18 56,000	Damaged in 1908 fire and boiler used on No. 2.
2nd 4	Charles L. Beach	4-4-0	Schenectady #46645	1909	49 13x18 57,000	Replacement for 1st No. 4. On final roster. Sold by Railway Equipment Co., 1920 to Oak Grove & Georgetown R. R. (Alabama).
5	Alfred Van Santvoord	4-4-0	Rogers #51126	1912	49 13x18 59,000	On final roster. Sold by Railway Equipment Co., 1920 to Oak Grove & Georgetown R. R. (Alabama).

Sources: Catskill Recorder, C. M. R.R. Correspondence, C. M. R.R. Sale List, Receiver's Affidavit, Robinson.

No. 1, the S. SHERWOOD DAY in 1883. In this very early photograph, the Catskill Mountain Railroad's first locomotive perches atop the piles driven in the swamp near the landing. *(Author's Collection)*

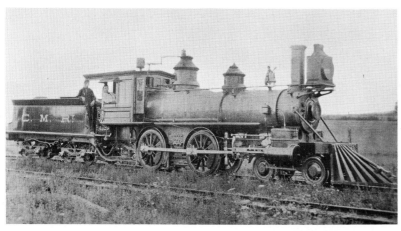

No. 1 in 1885. Apparently the original smokestack was found unsatisfactory, and this one replaced it. Note that the company name is now "railway." *(Gerald Best Collection)*

No. 2 at Cairo. Engineer Ruf (at right) and his fireman could be proud of the spotless locomotive in their charge. *(Charles Cammer Collection)*

No. 3 in 1910. Although the ALFRED VAN SANTVOORD retained its fluted domes (Nos. 1 and 2 did not), the smokestack has been reduced in diameter, probably reflecting John Driscoll's concern for draft and combustion, The name change to CHARLES T. VAN SANTVOORD was made after No. 5 was ordered. *(Fred Saunders Collection)*

130

First No. 4, the CHARLES L. BEACH. The first of two Schenectady locomotives purchased by the C. M. Ry., this fourth engine was needed when the shale brick business started. *(Alan Ruf Collection)*

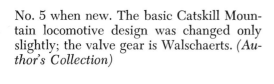

Second No. 4. As late as 1909, when this eight-wheeler was delivered, the railway retained the easily maintained Stephenson valve gear. *(Winfield W. Robinson Collection at Colgate University)*

No. 5 when new. The basic Catskill Mountain locomotive design was changed only slightly; the valve gear is Walschaerts. *(Author's Collection)*

Below, No. 5 is on the turntable. The railroad's most modern engine was turned around by man's oldest force — muscle power. *(Author's Collection)*

No. 5 goes logging. On the Oak Grove & George-town, the transplanted VAN SANTVOORD received a new low speed driving mechanism, planetary gears similar to Henry Ford's Model T transmission. (*Author's collection*).

C. & T. 2nd No. 2. Lacking the grace and simplicity of line of C. M. Ry. power, this 1901 Baldwin nevertheless looked sturdy and business-like. (*H. K. Vollrath Collection*)

2nd No. 2 at rest. With her fire banked, No. 2 awaits the new day and the latest Catskill visitors. No comparable photos of 2nd No. 1 have been located, although a head-on shot may be found elsewhere in the book. (*Author's collection*)

Ex-C. & T. 2nd No. 2. On the narrow-gauge division of the Milwaukee Road in Iowa, a Catskill locomotive finds work far from home. (*Gerald M. Best Collection*)

132

No.	Name	Type	Builder & No.	Date	Specifications	Service & Disposition
1		2-6-0	Brooks #464	1880	36 15x18 49,960	From Colorado & Southern #16. Retired about 1907 and boiler installed in Catskill Mountain House.
2		2-6-0	Brooks #465	1880	36 15x18 49,960	From Colorado & Southern #2. Out of service after 1900.
2nd 1	Isaac Pruyn	2-6-0	Baldwin #32715	1908	42 14x20 63,000	Sold to Birmingham Rail and Locomotive Co., 1924 for $1,750. to Bellevue & Cascade No. 3, then C. M. St. P. & P. No. 2.
2nd 2	Alfred V. S. Olcott	2-6-0	Baldwin #18884	1901	42 14x20 63,000	Replaced 1st No. 2. Sold to Birmingham Rail and Locomotive Co., 1924 for $1,750. to Bellevue & Cascade No. 2 then C. M. St. P. & P. No. 3.

NOTE: Hauck and Richardson suggest four locomotives as C. & T. 1st #1 and 1st #2. These are Colorado Central #11/ Union Pacific, Denver & Gulf #153/ Colorado & Southern #2, C. C. #12/ U. P. D. & G. #154/ C. & S. #3, C. C. #10/ U. P. D. & G. #152/ C. & S. #16, and C. C. #13/ U. P. D. & G. #155/ C. & S. #14. U. P. D. & G. Nos. 153 and 154 were smashed in a staged wreck in 1896 and then rebuilt.

Company records give no clues as to the acquisition, identification and disposal of 1st #1 and 1st #2 so the compiled data (construction numbers, dates and specifications) cannot be regarded as authenticated fact. Since the Ulster & Delaware standardgauged its Kaat-erskill branch and thus forced the Catskill & Tannersville to begin its own narrow gauge operation, it might be reasonable to assume that these first two engines came from the Kaaterskill stable. However, this "missing link" in their history has not been found.

2nd #1 and 2nd #2 were shipped to the yards of the Hoisting Machinery Company, Townley, New Jersey, in November of 1919 for storage and inspection by buyers.

Sources: C. M. R. R. Correspondence, C. M. R. R. Sale List, Hauck, Kindig, Richardson, Robinson.

C. & T. 1st No. 1 at Otis Summit. This is the only known photograph of either of the secondhand moguls. The company's 1904 financial report shows that an old boiler was sold for $102, probably a remnant of No. 2. *(Author's collection).*

No. 7 at the Landing. This is one of the original pieces of rolling stock for the C. M. Ry. Notice cabless engine No. 2 at left rear, the damage caused by the August, 1910 wreck. *(Photo by Harry Jones)*

No. 16 below at Wilmington in 1893. This Jackson & Sharp print shows one of the later, longer (by a few inches) cars owned by the company. The body has been mounted on standard-gauge trucks for shipment. *(Delaware State Archives)*

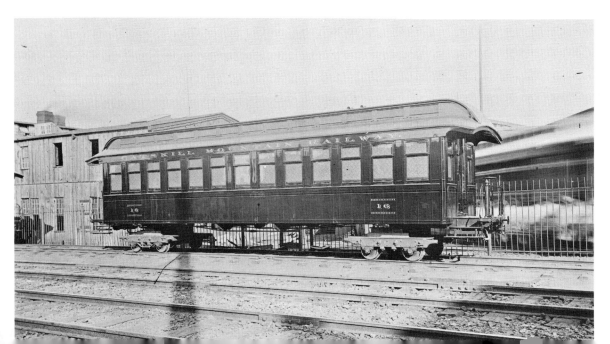

Appendix B

PASSENGER AND FREIGHT EQUIPMENT ROSTERS

The little that is known about Canajoharie & Catskill equipment is given in the text of this book.

Practically all records on rolling stock of the three narrow-gauge railroads were destroyed by fire in 1908. However, sufficient newspaper references and later sales records exist so that a rudimentary listing can be made.

Apparently most, if not all, of the original equipment was still on railroad property at the time of dissolution. The first passenger coaches of the Catskill Mountain Railway were delivered in traditional green livery with salmon colored vestibules. However, at some later time, the color scheme was changed to a wine or maroon for passenger cars, matching the freight equipment.

PASSENGER EQUIPMENT C. M. RY.

No.	Type	Length	Seats or Capacity	Builder & Date
1	Baggage	40' 10"	12 tons	Jackson & Sharp 1882
2	Baggage	40' 10"	12 tons	Jackson & Sharp 1882
3	Baggage	40' 10"	12 tons	Jackson & Sharp 1882
4	Baggage	40' 10"	12 tons	Jackson & Sharp 1882
5	Passenger	40' 3"	50 (cane)	Jackson & Sharp 1882
6	Passenger	40'	44 (plush)	Jackson & Sharp 1882
7	Passenger	40' 10"	44 (plush)	Jackson & Sharp 1882
8	Passenger	40' 10"	44 (plush)	Jackson & Sharp 1882
9	Passenger	40' 3"	52 (cane) (con-	Jackson & Sharp 1882
10	Passenger	40' 3"	verted in 1886 from	Jackson & Sharp 1882
11	Passenger	40' 3"	excursion seating)	Jackson & Sharp 1882
12	Excursion	40' 3"	Wooden seats	Jackson & Sharp 1882
13	Excursion	40' 3"	lengthwise	Jackson & Sharp 1882
14	Excursion	40' 3"	of car.	Jackson & Sharp 1882
15	Passenger	40' 3"	46 (plush)	Jackson & Sharp 1893
16	Passenger	40' 10"	46 (plush)	Jackson & Sharp 1893

PASSENGER EQUIPMENT C. & T. RY.

No.	Type	Length	Seats or Capacity	Builder & Date
1	Passenger		58 (plush)	Purchased
2	Passenger		58 (plush)	used
3	Combination		38	1899

PASSENGER EQUIPMENT OTIS RY.

Name	Type	Length	Seats or Capacity	Builder & Date
Rickerson Van	Passenger	46'	75	Jackson & Sharp 1892
Santvoord	Passenger	46'	75	Jackson & Sharp 1892

Disposition: Twelve passenger cars and three baggage cars sold to the National Railways of Mexico in April, 1920. Three C. & T. coaches at Laurel House Station were sold for $2,150 to a South American Buyer in September, 1919.

An Otis train. With its baggage car attached, the Otis car became a practical conveyance for people and things up the mountainside. (*Author's collection*)

An Otis car at the factory. Pity the sozzled citizen who might mistake this slanted conveyance for a local streetcar. (*Eleutherian Mills-Hagley Foundation*)

FREIGHT EQUIPMENT C. M. RY.

No.	Type	Length	Capacity	Builder & Date
1	Flat	30′	12 tons	Jackson & Sharp 1882
2	Flat	30′ 4″	12 tons	Jackson & Sharp 1882
3	Flat	30′ 6″	12 tons	Jackson & Sharp 1882
4	Gondola	30′ 8″	12 tons	Jackson & Sharp 1882
5	Flat	30′ 9″	12 tons	Jackson & Sharp 1882
6	Flat	30′ 6″	12 tons	Jackson & Sharp 1882
7	Gondola	31′	12 tons	Jackson & Sharp 1882
8	Gondola	31′	12 tons	Jackson & Sharp 1882
9	Flat	31′	12 tons	Jackson & Sharp 1882
10	Gondola	31′	12 tons	Jackson & Sharp 1882
11	Box	30′	15 tons	Jackson & Sharp 1882
12	Caboose	24′	12 tons	Jackson & Sharp 1882 (Converted from box)
13	Box	24′ 2″	12 tons	Jackson & Sharp 1893
14	Box	24′ 3″	12 tons	Jackson & Sharp 1893

Disposition: Certain unidentified freight cars were sold to North State Lumber Company on July 30, 1924 for $225. Flat cars #1, 2, and 3 and Caboose #12 were still at the Point in 1922.

FREIGHT EQUIPMENT OTIS RY.

No.	Type	Length	Capacity
1	Box	22′	8 tons
2	Box	22′	8 tons
3	Gondola	22′	8 tons
4	Gondola	22′	8 tons
15	Gondola	22′	8 tons
16	Gondola	22′	8 tons
17	Box	22′	8 tons
18	Box	22′	8 tons

All Otis cars were equipped with Eames Vacuum and N. Y. Air Brake equipment so that they could run on either C. & T. or C. M. Ry. trains.

FREIGHT EQUIPMENT C. & T. RY.

No.	Type	Length	Capacity	Builder & Date
3	Box		10 tons	Origin unknown. Probably built or rebuilt at Catskill shops.
	Flat		10 tons	″

Sources: *Catskill Examiner,* C. M. R. R. Sales List, C. M. R. R. Correspondence.

An Otis gondola. The cargo here is a wrecked auto being sent to Catskill from Haines Corners via all three little railroads. *(Winfield W. Robinson Collection at Colgate University)*

Charles Addison Beach at 60. C. L.'s
nephew was long associated with the
railroad network in various responsible positions. *(Mrs. Charles A. W.
Beach Collection)*

George H., son of Charles L. Beach.
When C. A. Beach died in 1913,
George H. became president of the
Catskill Mountain Railway. *(Mrs. Mary
Van Wagonen Rising Collection)*

Thomas E. Jones, at left, served in
several capacities on the railroads, pri-
marily as freight and passenger agent,
but also as the liquidating receiver for
the lines. *(Harry Jones Collection)*

Appendix C

ROSTER OF OFFICIALS AND EMPLOYEES

The information supplied here is admittedly incomplete, particularly for the Canajoharie & Catskill Rail Road. The officers of this early line have been identified, for the most part, but little is known for certain about C. & C. employees. The text of this book gives the few employee names that have been located.

The employee lists for the C. M., Otis, and C. & T. lines have been compiled as carefully as possible, but since complete company records are lacking and memories of surviving employees are sometimes faulty, there may be a few unintentional omissions.

Although these three later railroads were separate corporations, they were controlled by the same group of men. The proprietors of the Catskill Mountain House and the owners of the Hudson River Day Line were substantial investors, and they were well represented in the administration of these narrow-gauge lines. The three railroads shared a common office in Catskill and operating employees were often shifted from one line to another. In 1916 and until abandonment, the three were reorganized and operated under one corporate name, the Catskill Mountain Railroad.

Canajoharie & Catskill
Presidents: Thomas B. Cooke, Ezra Hawley
Secretaries: Amos Cornwall, Luke Kiersted
Treasurer: Peter T. Mesick
Chief Engineers: Ephraim Beach, Thomas Falls
Receiver: John T. Mann

Catskill Mountain
Presidents: Charles L. Beach, Alfred Van Santvoord, Charles A. Beach, George H. Beach
Vice Presidents: Isaac Pruyn, Charles L. Beach, W. J. Jennings
Treasurer: Orrin Day
Secretary: Samuel L. Penfield
General Superintendents and Secretaries: Charles A. Beach, T. E. Jones
General Freight and Passenger Agent: Thomas E. Jones
General Superintendent: T. E. Jones
Master Mechanic: John P. Driscoll
Receivers: George H. Beach and Thomas E. Jones (1915-1918), Thomas E. Jones (1919)

Cairo
Presidents: Lewis Wolfe, A. V. S. Olcott, C. L. Rickerson
Vice President: J. D. Hasbrouck
Secretary-Treasurer: W. J. Hughes
Secretary: Samuel Harris
Treasurer: Frederick Hill

Otis
Presidents: Charles L. Rickerson, A. V. S. Olcott
Vice Presidents: W. D. Baldwin, Charles T. Van Santvoord
Secretary-Treasurer: C. C. Hager
Secretary: W. Y. Hawley
Treasurer: T. E. Jones
General Superintendent: Charles A. Beach
Receiver: Thomas E. Jones

Catskill & Tannersville
Presidents: Charles L. Rickerson, A. V. S. Olcott
Vice Presidents: Charles L. Beach, James Stead
Secretary-Treasurer: Charles A. Beach
Secretary: W. Y. Hawley
Treasurer: T. E. Jones
Receivers: William Y. Hawley, Thomas E. Jones
Office Staff: Harry E. Jones, Clerk
Mary A. Decker, Stenographer

EMPLOYEE ROSTER
CATSKILL MOUNTAIN

Engineers

John L. Driscoll	Edward Warner
John Craig	Claude Heath
William H. Driscoll	William Coffin
William Shufelt	Jesse Oakley
Francis Ruf	L. R. McGlashan
Charles F. Long	Addison Edwards

Firemen

Walter Finch	Wesley Lewis
Richard Covell	Lewis Freese
Edward Staples	F. Scott
Michael Cimorelli	William Felter
Kinsley Parkes	Harry Philes
Hiland Holmes	Millard Jerome
Edward Loveland	Fred Prediger

Conductors

W. Irving Osborn	Ward Bogardus
George Hanford	Sheldon Lane
William Whitcomb	Del Utter
William Bogardus	Frank L. Vedder
Martin Brewer	James B. Tolley
Burr Vaughn	

Switchmen

Robert Osterhout	M. VanLoan
Charles Halcott	George Richter

C. M. Ry. employees at the engine house. From left to right, rear row: Engineer Frank J. Ruf, Master Mechanic John L. Driscoll, Switchman George Richter. Front row: Engineer William H. Driscoll, Engineer Jesse Oakley, Carpenter James Salisbury, Engineer Charles Long, Car Knocker Robert Osterhout. *(Winfield W. Robinson Collection at Colgate University)*

C. & T. track gang, below, at North Lake. *(Elmer Mower Collection)*

At left, Otis Conductor Elmer Mower at the Ledge.
(Elmer Mower Collection)

The Otis tower. Roy McGlashan appears at the window.
(Elmer Mower Collection)

140

Trackmen

William Teal	Patrick Ryan
F. North	Martin Hart

Trainmen & Baggage Masters

Edward Steenburn	Frank L. Vedder
Arthur Dowling	Charles Lockwood
J. B. Wolcott	John Hulbert
Will Covell	Addison Groat
Herbert Rockefeller	H. M. Moore
R. Elliot	R. Halcott
C. Ostrom	B. L. Chichester
J. Cole	Peter Timmerman
Lester Thorn	George Richter
James P. Tolley	William Duston
Dennis Holmes	Burton L. Edwards
A. W. Phillips	Joseph Nealis
Ralph Ruland	Robert Coffin
Chester Stewart	Sherman Earl
Abram Felter	Elton Cummings
Henry Kells	John Bordt
Percy Gardner	Ward Bogardus

Agents

Catskill Landing — Percy W. Decker, Harry J. Fox, M. Harry Hill, C. Garrison. (Helpers: Van Duncan, Robert Coffin)

Catskill Village — A. A. Cole, Goodwin Cowles, Clifford Dykeman. (Helpers: James Cunningham, Frank Rockefeller)

West Shore — W. H. Thorne, James Beach

South Cairo — J. B. Phinney, Chauncy Wolcott

Cairo — E. S. Freese, Ira Tolley

Otis Junction — George Wolfert, A. Griffin

Palenville — W. A. Gardner, A. Griffin

CATSKILL & TANNERSVILLE

Engineers

Edward Warner	G. H. Craft
Charles Greene	Claude Heath
Wesley Greene	

Firemen

H. Cole	Wesley Lewis
E. Newkirk	

Conductors

Percy H. Gardner	Herbert O'Hara
James H. Layman	Charles Blackett

Trainmen & Baggage Masters

H. Hommell	E. Taylor
S. Greene	Howard Humphrey
W. Bogart	Arthur Dowling
J. B. North	

Blacksmith
Christopher Newkirk

Trackman
Frank North

Agents

Otis Summit (Mountain House) — C. W. Garrison, T. R. Hargreaves, J. Fray, M. Harry Hill

Haines Corners — William Carnright, William Ryan

Tannersville — John O'Hara, George Backman

OTIS

Engineers

Allen Banks	W. H. Driscoll
S. Parsell	

Towermen

James Halcott	Howard Crapser
Ed Goodwin	L. R. McGlashan

Brakemen & Baggage Masters

W. E. Howard	Charles Stewart
E. Taylor	Alvin Folk
August Graf	

Fireman
C. Howard

Conductors

John Myers	Victor Howard
Carson Edwards	William Whitcomb
Elmer Mower	

Trackmen

Henry Morton	John Graf

Sources: *Annual Reports of the Board of Railroad Commissioners of the State of New York, Catskill Examiner, Catskill Recorder*, Coffin, Jones, Payroll records (1915-1917), Wolcott.

The Catskill ticket office in 1914. In the Village Station are, from left to right, Lee Terwilliger, Goodwin Cowles, Agent Al Cole and James Cunningham. The waiting room is just beyond the ticket window behind Cole and the general office for the railroads is upstairs. Note the telephone and the absence of telegraph equipment; the railroad depended on a phone system for all its messages. *(Ruf Collection)*

Tannersville. This picture is said to be of the last year of
C. & T. operation. Conductor O'Hara consults his watch,
but no one seems to be in a hurry. *(Author's Collection)*

Index

All textual and illustrative matter has been listed here, with the exception of the notes and the appendices. The listed items will lead the reader to the appropriate related notes; the appendices are concentrated compilations of information on personnel and equipment readily accessible to the reader.

* The asterisk indicates an illustration

143

PALENVILLE